Street-Smart Management Wisdom

Wisdom

Management Without BS

Richard Lowe

The Writing King

Street-Smart Management Wisdom: Management Without BS

Copyright © 2026 by Richard G Lowe

Table of Contents

See books by Richard Lowe at
https://masterofworlds.com

Get free publishing insights and industry updates at
https://thewritingking.substack.com

For ghostwriting and book coaching services see
https://thewritingking.com

A Note on Structure

This book was deliberately built around the StoryBrand framework developed by Donald Miller.

StoryBrand is a messaging and narrative framework grounded in the mechanics of story: a hero faces a problem, encounters a villain that makes the problem worse, finds a guide who gives them a plan, takes action, and is transformed by the outcome. Applied to business communication and nonfiction, it produces writing that readers experience rather than observe.

Most management books are written from the outside in: here is a principle, here is evidence for it, here is how to apply it. The reader is a student receiving instruction. StoryBrand reverses this. The reader is the hero. The characters in the book are guides who have already faced what the reader is about to face. The framework is the plan. The transformation is what becomes possible when the plan is executed.

In this book, Maya Delacroix, David Rodriguez, and Keisha Williams function simultaneously as heroes in their own stories and as guides for yours. You watch them fail in ways you will recognize, find the frameworks that resolve their specific problem, and arrive transformed at the end of each chapter. The transformation is the template. The details of their situations are not the point. The shape of the problem and the shape of the resolution are.

Each chapter is structured around five StoryBrand beats: the villain (the specific force working against the character), the stakes (what fails if they don't solve it), the guide (the person who arrives with the framework), the plan (the specific named methodology the guide provides), and the transformation (the before and after that closes each chapter). The action items at the end of each chapter are the reader's version of the plan.

If you are a ghostwriting client evaluating this book as a sample of what I do: this structure is not accidental and it is not decorative. It is the architecture that makes management content readable rather than merely informative. The StoryBrand framework can be applied to any business nonfiction — memoir, thought leadership, how-to, case study — and produces the same result: a reader who finishes the book having experienced a transformation rather than attended a lecture.

The three characters in this book have distinct voices, distinct cultural backgrounds, and distinct ways of encountering the same management challenges. That diversity of perspective is also deliberate. A management book that speaks to one kind of manager speaks to a fraction of its potential audience. A book that shows three different people arriving at the same hard-won understanding speaks to almost everyone who has ever been handed responsibility they didn't fully feel ready for.

That's the book you're holding. I hope it's useful. — Richard Lowe

Introduction: The Management Revolution

Nobody warned me that becoming a manager would feel like being handed the keys to a spaceship and told to figure out how to fly it while already in orbit. One day I was debugging code and architecting systems. The next I was trying to figure out why two engineers who sat six feet apart in a Slack channel had somehow developed the kind of mutual resentment that required a mediator, a retrospective, and a conversation I had no idea how to have.

When I first became a manager in 1981, the biggest challenge was delegating work to people who sat ten feet away. Fast forward to now, and I'm writing this book because everything we thought we knew about management has been turned upside down, shaken vigorously, and handed back to us by people who never had to manage anything more complex than their Netflix queue.

The traditional management playbook assumed you could read body language, have impromptu hallway conversations, and build culture through shared coffee and proximity. That playbook is now roughly as useful as a fax machine. We're all figuring this out as we go. Some of us have just been doing it longer and made more spectacular mistakes along the way.

Meet Your Guides

This book follows three managers navigating real challenges in real organizations. You'll follow their stories across fourteen chapters, watching them fail, adapt, and eventually figure it out. They're not archetypes. They're people.

Maya Delacroix is twenty-six, first-generation Haitian-American, raised in Miami. Her father's an electrician, her mother does medical billing, and Maya got into engineering on a scholarship by being the person who solved problems other people gave up on. She's precise, self-contained, and constitutionally incapable of asking for help before she's exhausted every other option. She was one of the best engineers at FinTechFlow. Then her manager quit and everyone assumed she'd be fine. She was not fine, at first. What she did about that is most of this book.

David Rodriguez is thirty-four, third-generation Mexican-American, raised in San Antonio. His grandfather ran a restaurant, his father sells insurance, his mother teaches middle school, and David learned early that warmth is a skill. He's the person who remembers your kid's name, buys tacos when the team ships something, and managed his creative team at Meridian Marketing for five years by being likable and getting out of the way. It worked beautifully until it didn't. The week everything broke simultaneously is Chapter 2. The version of David who comes out the other side is a different manager.

Keisha Williams is fifty-two, Black Southern, raised in Birmingham. Her grandmother marched. Her mother was a union steward for thirty years. Keisha grew up understanding how institutions work from the inside — who actually holds power, where decisions really get made, why some things last and others don't. She's been running operations at Meridian Manufacturing for fifteen years. She is, by any measure, excellent at her job. That excellence turns out to have a shadow side. It took a vacation that went badly wrong for her to see it.

The Death of Command and Control

The old model of management was simple: smart people at the top made decisions, communicated them downward, and everyone else executed the plan. Problems bubbled up slowly. Change happened at a pace that allowed for lengthy committee discussions and proper change management processes.

This worked when business moved slowly, technology changed gradually, and everyone showed up to the same building. It falls apart completely when your company needs to pivot strategy every quarter, your best developer is working from Lisbon, and your newest hire expects to have input on major decisions within their first month.

I learned this the hard way at Trader Joe's, where I spent nearly two decades managing technical operations in a company that prided itself on moving fast. The managers who succeeded weren't the ones with the best org charts. They were the ones who could make good decisions with incomplete information, build trust with people they rarely saw, and help their teams navigate constant change without losing their minds.

What This Book Won't Do

It won't tell you management is easy or that there's a formula. It won't give you a leadership philosophy that requires personality traits you don't have. It won't pretend that the hard parts get easier. They don't. What changes is your capacity to handle them.

It also won't fill pages with hypotheticals and composite scenarios. The situations Maya, David, and Keisha face are drawn from real management failures — mine and others'. The details have been changed. The mistakes haven't been softened.

What This Book Will Do

It will help you become the kind of manager you would want to work for. That's the whole goal. Everything else — the frameworks, the action items, the before-and-after chapter endings — is in service of that.

Each chapter follows one of the three characters through a specific management challenge. The challenge has a villain: a force, a gap, a bad instinct working against them. It has stakes: what fails if they don't figure it out. It has a guide: someone who's been where they are and has a framework that actually works. And it ends with a transformation — a before and after that shows you what changed and why.

The action items at the end of each chapter are the reader's version of the plan. Three things you can do this week. Not theory. Practice.

How to Use This Book

You don't have to read it in order. If you're dealing with a performance issue right now, go to Chapter 5. If you're about to make your first hire, start with Chapter 3. If your boss is making your life miserable, Chapter 8 is waiting for you.

That said, the characters develop across chapters. Reading straight through, you'll watch Maya, David, and Keisha grow in ways that make the later chapters hit harder. The choice is yours.

Your Management Journey Starts Here

The transition from individual contributor to manager is one of the hardest career moves you'll make. The skills that got you promoted are not the skills the new job requires. Nobody tells you this clearly enough, early enough.

Maya, David, and Keisha figured it out. Not gracefully. Not fast. But they figured it out, and the path they took is navigable. The sticky note is still on Maya's monitor. The abuelo's advice is still ringing in David's ears. Keisha's documentation is still in the third drawer, under principles.

Let's begin.

Chapter 1: Maya's Promotion - The New Manager's Reality Check

Maya Delacroix accepted the Engineering Team Lead role on a Tuesday, ran a risk analysis on it by Wednesday, and by Thursday had a spreadsheet mapping her six direct reports' known strengths, estimated learning curves, and communication preferences based on Slack response patterns and code review history. She was twenty-six. She thought she was ready.

Jake — her manager, the one who'd just quit to join his fourth startup — told her she'd be fine. He said this in a twelve-minute meeting that covered roughly half of what she needed to know, which was Jake's way. She wrote down everything he said. She did not write down what he didn't say, which turned out to be the problem.

What Jake didn't say: that managing engineers is nothing like engineering. That a team isn't a distributed system. That you cannot grep a human being for the source of their problem and push a patch.

Three months in, she was up at eleven PM, Haitian coffee going cold beside her laptop, staring at a Slack thread that had somehow evolved from a question about code formatting into a referendum on whether Marcus in Chicago respected Nora in Prague, and she was thinking: nobody warned me. Nobody warned me once.

The Technical Skills Trap

The Alex meeting was on a Thursday at 2 PM, and Maya had prepared for it the way she prepared for everything: with data.

Three weeks of commit history. Task estimates mapped against actual delivery. A chart showing the delta widening over time. She had a root cause hypothesis — context-switching from two overlapping projects — and a proposed fix. The meeting was scheduled for thirty minutes. She expected to use twenty.

Alex looked at the chart for a long moment. Then he said: "I'm not a system you can debug."

Maya kept her expression neutral. She'd learned to do that in rooms where being visibly rattled was expensive. "I'm not treating you like a system," she said. "I'm trying to understand what's happening so I can help."

"You presented me with a performance dashboard," Alex said. "In a one-on-one. That's not help. That's a case for the prosecution."

He wasn't wrong. She knew he wasn't wrong approximately four seconds after he said it, which meant she spent the remaining twenty-six minutes of the meeting knowing she'd made a mistake she couldn't undo because she hadn't prepared for this version of the conversation.

She had optimized for the wrong outcome. She'd diagnosed the technical problem and ignored the human one, which in this case was the technical problem.

That night she sat at her kitchen table with a cold Haitian coffee and wrote in her notes app: Alex wasn't underperforming. Alex needed his manager to ask how he was doing. I gave him a regression chart instead. Then: What else am I misreading?

The answer, she would spend the next three months finding out, was almost everything.

The Distributed Team Problem

The team was quieter than it used to be. Maya had logged this as "more focused." It was not more focused.

She was tracking the wrong things — meeting efficiency, response times, ticket velocity. These numbers told her the team was functional. What they didn't tell her: Nora in Prague had stopped contributing ideas in large group calls three weeks ago, and Marcus Oduya in Chicago had started solving problems himself rather than surfacing them because surfacing problems had started leading to forty-minute Zoom discussions that resolved nothing.

Maya's first fix was very Maya: she redesigned the meeting structure. Agendas twenty-four hours in advance. Speaking time allocated by agenda item. Recordings posted within the hour. The meetings became more organized. The quiet got worse.

Nora told her why, finally, in a one-on-one Maya had almost cancelled. She said that her English under pressure in a fast-moving group of native speakers was different from her regular English, and that she'd rather stay silent than say something wrong and confirm whatever people already assumed about her.

Marcus told her something different but related: he'd stopped flagging blockers because the last three times he had, Maya jumped in and solved them herself. "It's faster when you do it," he said. "But I feel like I'm watching someone else run my job."

Two people. Two completely different problems. One symptom: silence.

The thing about managing a distributed team, Maya wrote that night, is that you cannot see the silence. In an office you feel it. On a Slack channel it looks like productivity. She stopped optimizing the meetings and started asking different questions: what would make it easier for you to speak up? The answers weren't scalable. She implemented them individually anyway.

The Peer-to-Manager Transition

Alex had been her closest colleague for two years before she became his manager. They'd eaten lunch together three or four times a week, complained about the same things, covered for each other during crunch. She'd thought that history would make the transition easier.

It made it harder in a way she hadn't anticipated.

The tension broke over a maintenance project he didn't want to take on. He pushed back — reasonably, she thought, she'd have done the same six months ago — and she held the line because she'd learned by then that she had to. He looked at her across the video call like she'd done something to him personally.

"You care more about the company than about us now," he said.

She almost said that's not true. She stopped herself. Because in some sense it was true. Her obligations were different now. She had to weigh team interests against organizational ones in a way she hadn't before, and pretending otherwise wasn't going to help either of them.

"I care about the team," she said carefully. "That's why I need this project to get done, and you're the right person for it. I know that's not what you want to hear."

Alex was quiet. "This is weird," he said finally.

"Yes," Maya said. "It is weird."

It didn't fix things between them. But it was the first honest conversation they'd had since the promotion, and honest was somewhere to build from.

The Delegation Trap

An integration project came in at the wrong time — they were already at capacity — and Maya's instinct was to take it herself. She was faster. She knew the codebase. She could do in three days what would take anyone else two weeks.

She did exactly that. She delivered it on time. It worked correctly.

During the retrospective, Marcus pointed out that he'd essentially watched her solo a project the team should have owned. "I learned nothing," he said. "You learned nothing about what we can do. And we're exactly as dependent on you as we were before."

She had optimized for output. She had not built capacity. She'd been confusing those two things for months, and it explained why her team kept waiting for her to solve things instead of solving them.

Her next move was deliberate and uncomfortable: she assigned Nora to lead the technical design for a new feature. Made herself available for questions, not direction. Then sat on her hands for two weeks while Nora made choices Maya wouldn't have made.

The result worked. It wasn't how Maya would have done it. That was not the same as wrong.

Nora presented at the team review with a confidence that hadn't been there three months ago. She'd earned something real. Maya had gotten out of the way long enough for that to happen. It was the most useful thing she'd done all month, and she hadn't done anything at all.

The Communication Protocol Problem

The next crisis was invisible until it wasn't. Marcus was checking Slack constantly and responding within minutes. Nora had different hours and a different idea of what "available" meant. Neither of them had told Maya, and Maya hadn't asked, because she'd assumed everyone operated on the same defaults.

They didn't. By the time she noticed, Marcus quietly resented Nora for what he read as unresponsiveness, and Nora had no idea anything was wrong.

Maya convened a team conversation she'd been putting off because she hadn't known how to frame it: not a performance discussion, not a meeting about the meeting, but an explicit negotiation about how the team communicated. Core hours. Response time expectations by channel. Which things were urgent and which just felt urgent at 11 PM.

The conversation took ninety minutes and produced a one-page document. That document ended more ambient team friction than anything else she did that quarter. The problem had never been a people problem. It had been an unspoken-expectations problem, which looked identical to a people problem until you named it.

What Sarah Braddock Told Her

Maya called Sarah Braddock on a Sunday afternoon — the time she reserved for calls she'd been putting off because she didn't know how to start them.

Sarah had managed her at her previous job and was now a VP at a larger company. She was one of the few people Maya trusted enough to be wrong in front of.

"I can't tell if I'm actually bad at this or just at the bottom of a learning curve," Maya said. "From inside it they look the same."

"Describe the thing you'd most like to undo," Sarah said.

Maya described the Alex meeting. The chart. The prosecution metaphor.

Sarah was quiet for a moment. Then: "You just switched jobs. Not roles — jobs. The skills that got you promoted are not the skills the new job requires. Engineers build things. Managers build the conditions for other people to build things. Those are genuinely different activities, and your instincts are still engineer instincts."

"I know that conceptually," Maya said.

"Right. Conceptually it's obvious. But when Alex was underperforming, your brain said: gather data, diagnose, fix. That's correct for a broken system. Alex wasn't a broken system. Alex had feelings about something, and you needed to find out what they were before you did anything else."

"So what's the actual framework?" Maya said. Because Maya always wanted the framework.

Sarah said: "People-first, problem-second. Every time. Before you present data, before you diagnose, before you propose a solution — find out what they're experiencing. Not as a step you get through to reach the real conversation. As the real conversation." She paused. "That's it. It doesn't feel like enough because it isn't a system. You like systems."

"I do like systems," Maya said.

"I know. The irony is that if you apply that one principle consistently, your team will function like a better system than anything you could design directly. People perform better when they feel understood. That's not soft. That's just how they're built."

Maya wrote: People-first, problem-second. Every time. She put it on a sticky note on her monitor. It was still there six months later, coffee-stained on one edge, slightly curled at the corner.

Maya's 90-Day Reckoning

Thirty days in, she was reactive. Responding to everything, initiating nothing, running on caffeine and the fear of being visibly bad at something.

Sixty days in, she started tracking how she spent her time and found that roughly forty percent of it was solving problems her team could have handled without her — because she'd made herself the path of least resistance. She started stopping herself from answering. The first time, she watched a question come into Slack and just didn't respond for three hours. Her hand moved toward the keyboard twice. She went and made coffee instead.

The person figured it out. She mentioned this to Sarah that weekend. Sarah said: "And you're surprised?"

Ninety days in, she wasn't the same manager she'd been at thirty days. She wasn't good yet — she was clear-eyed enough to know that — but the shape of the job was visible to her now in a way it hadn't been. She could see what she was trying to build, even when she was building it badly.

The real marker came from Alex. He came to her with a complex architecture problem — not expecting her to solve it, asking for help thinking through it. Two hours on a shared whiteboard, neither of them writing code, both of them thinking out loud. She produced nothing at the end of it except a person who left with clarity he hadn't had walking in.

She sat with that. Then she wrote in her notes: This is what the job actually is. Building the conditions. Not building the thing.

Before and After

Before: Maya Delacroix managed her team the way she'd architected her systems — logically, efficiently, with total control over every variable. When people didn't behave like systems she gathered more data. When the data didn't help she worked harder. She was six months into the job before she understood why neither of those was the right response.

After: She still gathered data. Still ran one-on-ones with structured agendas, still kept a spreadsheet on skills and learning trajectories. The difference was she asked before diagnosing, listened before proposing, and stayed out of the way long enough for people to surprise her. Her team was not optimized. It was alive, which turned out to be more useful.

Your First Week Actions

Schedule individual listening sessions — not one-on-ones with agendas, conversations. Ask each person: what's working, what's frustrating you, what do you wish your manager understood about your work? Do not problem-solve. Do not present data. Listen.

For one week, log every time you step in to solve something. At the end of the week, mark which ones required you and which your team could have handled. The ratio will be instructive and probably uncomfortable.

Find your Sarah Braddock — a mentor or former manager who has made this transition and will tell you the truth about what you're getting wrong. The peer-to-manager shift is too disorienting to navigate alone.

Maya figured it out. It wasn't elegant, and it wasn't fast. The sticky note is still on her monitor.

David Rodriguez had been doing this for five years and thought he'd already figured it out. He'd find out soon what "figured out" actually costs when five years of winging it runs into its first real test.

Chapter 2: David's Foundation Crisis - Building Your Leadership Operating System

Five years. David Rodriguez had been running the Meridian Marketing creative team for five years, and if you asked him how he did it, he'd tell you the same thing he told his wife, his abuelo, and anyone else who asked: you hire good people, you get out of their way, and you buy them tacos when they ship something.

That was not a management philosophy. He knew that now.

He found out in the same week in March that his biggest client announced they were bringing everything in-house, his best designer quit to freelance, and Meridian's newest hire froze up completely when the pressure hit. Three crises, no playbook. David sat at his kitchen table that Sunday night eating leftover enchiladas and thinking about how for five years the machine had just run, and he had no idea how.

"I've been winging it," he told his wife. She put her fork down. "I know," she said. Which was somehow worse.

The Illusion of Effortless Leadership

For five years, Meridian's creative team had run on what David privately called the taco principle: hire good people, get out of their way, and buy them tacos when they ship something. He said this out loud to new hires during onboarding, delivered with the easy confidence of someone whose approach had never been seriously tested.

He understood later that the taco principle was not a management philosophy. It was a description of what happens when nothing has gone wrong yet.

The week in March that everything went wrong at once: his biggest client announced they were bringing their marketing in-house. His best designer quit to freelance. His newest hire froze completely under the first real pressure she'd faced. Three crises, no playbook. David sat at his kitchen table that Sunday night eating leftover enchiladas and realizing that for five years the machine had just run, and he had genuinely no idea how.

"I've been winging it," he told his wife.

She put her fork down. "I know," she said.

Which was somehow the worst part.

The Overcorrection Trap

David's first instinct was to implement every management best practice he'd ever read about, all at once. Weekly team meetings. Individual development plans. Project tracking software. Mandatory retrospectives. A new communication protocol that he sent to the team in a 600-word email at 11 PM on a Tuesday.

His designer Zoe pulled him aside after a check-in that had somehow stretched to ninety minutes. "David," she said, "I've spent more time in meetings about my work this week than doing my work. Can we find somewhere between chaos and bureaucracy?"

He'd made the classic mistake: he'd confused activity with effectiveness. More meetings didn't mean better outcomes. More documentation didn't mean clearer thinking. He'd swapped one kind of disorder for another kind.

What he was missing was a framework for why any of it mattered. He wasn't building systems because the systems would make the team better. He was building systems because he was scared, and doing things felt better than sitting with the uncertainty.

He cancelled half the new meetings. He sent Zoe an apology that was two sentences long. He started over, slower this time, asking a question he should have asked from the beginning: what does this team actually need to do its best work?

Decision-Making Under Fire

The crisis exposed something David hadn't known was missing: he had no consistent process for making decisions under pressure. When he had time — which was most of the last five years — he'd gathered information, consulted informally, and made calls on instinct. It had worked because the stakes were manageable and the instincts were decent.

Under real pressure, instinct alone wasn't enough. He was treating a budget decision with the same urgency as a hiring one, and a client communication with the same deliberation as a long-term strategy question. Everything felt equally critical because he had no framework for telling them apart.

His new department head Carla gave him one, bluntly, during a check-in where she could see he was spinning. "Stop treating every decision like it's the same size," she said. "Ask yourself two things: how reversible is this, and what's the blast radius if I'm wrong? High reversibility and small blast radius — just decide. Low reversibility and large blast radius — slow down and get more information. Everything else falls somewhere in between."

David wrote it on a notecard and taped it to his monitor. He's not a notecard person generally. He made an exception.

The framework didn't make the decisions easier. It made them faster, which under crisis conditions was nearly as valuable. He stopped treating every call like it might end his career and started treating most of them like what they were: reversible, manageable, recoverable.

Managing Up: The Part He'd Been Ignoring

When Carla became his department head, David discovered that five years of keeping his head down had left him nearly invisible to senior leadership. Carla didn't know what his team was capable of. She didn't know what they'd built or what they'd saved. She'd inherited David as a name on an org chart.

He'd spent years focused entirely on his team and almost none on the organization around it. He'd thought good work would speak for itself. It doesn't. Good work needs someone to translate it into organizational language, and that someone is the manager.

He started showing up to optional leadership meetings. He started sending Carla a brief Friday update — not a status report, more like a short story about what the team was working on and why it mattered. He started asking her questions about organizational priorities instead of waiting for the priorities to arrive as directives.

It felt awkward at first, like being someone he wasn't. Then it started feeling like the job he actually had, as opposed to the smaller, more comfortable version of the job he'd been doing.

"I felt like I'd been playing manager," he said later, to his abuelo, who was not a management consultant but who had run a restaurant for thirty years and understood what David was describing exactly. "Turns out playing manager and being one are different things." His abuelo said: "Yeah, mijo. The restaurant taught me that."

The Systems Rebuild

Six months after the crisis, David had built something he hadn't had before: a minimal set of processes that gave him actual visibility into his team's work without requiring meetings about meetings to maintain them.

He called it minimum viable infrastructure. Not the system he'd imagined when he'd overcorrected, with its mandatory retros and 600-word emails. Just the lightest possible structure that answered the questions he actually needed answered: what's moving, what's stuck, what's about to become a problem?

A weekly fifteen-minute team sync. Individual check-ins every two weeks, not every week. A shared project tracker that everyone used because it was simple, not because it was mandated. A decision log that captured what was decided and why, so the next crisis wouldn't require him to reconstruct six months of context from memory.

None of it was sophisticated. That was the point. Sophisticated systems require a dedicated person to maintain them. David didn't have that. He had a creative team trying to make things, and the systems needed to serve the work, not compete with it.

What Carla Told Him

Carla said it directly, which was her way: "You're a decent manager who's been coasting on a stable environment. The environment stopped being stable. Now you're finding out who you actually are."

David had been ready to be defensive. Instead he just said: "That's fair."

She gave him the framework she'd used in her own career: distinguish between the things you're doing because they make your team better, and the things you're doing because they make you feel like a manager. The first category is your actual job. The second category is noise. Cut the noise, double down on the first category, and the rest mostly takes care of itself.

David thought about the taco principle. It was in the second category. It made him feel like a cool boss. It didn't make his team better at anything.

He still bought tacos sometimes. He just stopped thinking of it as a management strategy.

Before and After

Before: David Rodriguez managed by feel, by relationship, by the accumulated goodwill of five years of being a decent boss in a stable environment. When the environment destabilized, he had no infrastructure underneath him and no framework for building one fast enough.

After: He had systems — minimal, deliberate, actually used. He had a decision framework. He had a relationship with his department head that was based on genuine communication rather than staying out of each other's way. He was still charming, still warm, still the person who bought tacos at the right moment. He was also, finally, the person who could tell you exactly what was happening in his team and why, on any given Tuesday.

Your Systems Building Actions

Identify one decision type you've been handling inconsistently and write down the two questions: how reversible is this, and what's the blast radius? Apply them for thirty days and see if your decision-making speed improves.

Schedule a monthly conversation with your boss focused entirely on organizational priorities — not your team's status, but where the organization is going and how your team connects to it. Make it a conversation, not a report.

Build one piece of minimum viable infrastructure: the lightest possible system that gives you early visibility into a problem that's currently invisible until it blows up.

David's five years of winging it weren't wasted — the relationships he'd built, the instincts he'd developed, those were real. What he learned was that they weren't enough on their own. Instinct needs infrastructure to land on.

Maya was figuring out how to lead her first team from scratch. Six months in, she had one open headcount and a backlog eating her alive. She treated hiring the same way she treated every problem. The result would cost her four months and teach her more about the difference between credentials and capability than any textbook ever had.

Chapter 3: Maya's First Hire - Hiring for the Future

Six months in, Maya had exactly one open headcount and a backlog that was eating her alive. She treated the hiring process the way she treated every problem: systematically. She wrote a job description that was essentially a technical specification. She built a skills matrix. She designed a four-stage interview process with weighted scoring criteria.

She was thorough. She was rigorous. She was completely wrong about what she was selecting for.

"I want someone who can hit the ground running," Maya told her team during the kickoff meeting, and then proceeded to describe the perfect engineer for the problems they'd had eighteen months ago. His name was Connor Walsh — and she'd later describe him to Priya as proof that technical perfection and collaborative instincts have nothing to do with each other, as she would later tell Priya — and he had the exact resume she'd described. He aced every technical screen. He said all the right words about collaboration.

Four months later, Maya was debugging his code at midnight, trying to understand how someone so technically correct could be so organizationally destructive. She'd optimized for the wrong variable. Again.

The Technical Perfection Trap

The job description Maya wrote for FinTechFlow's first engineering hire was essentially a technical specification. Required skills: React, Node.js, PostgreSQL, Docker, AWS, microservices experience. Preferred: fintech domain knowledge and five or more years at a startup. She'd built a weighted scoring matrix for the interviews. She'd designed four stages with objective rubrics.

She was thorough. She was rigorous. She selected the wrong person.

His name was Connor Walsh — not her ex-manager Jake, a completely different person as she'd later tell Priya — and he had the exact credentials she'd described. Computer science degree from a recognized university. Five years at a company whose name she recognized. He answered every technical question correctly. He used the word "collaboration" four times in the final interview.

Four months later, Maya was at her kitchen table at midnight debugging his code, trying to understand how someone so technically correct could be so organizationally corrosive.

Connor's code was clean. His documentation was thorough. And he treated every pivot, every changed requirement, every request to work differently as a personal assault. When the product team adjusted the UI based on customer feedback, he rewrote the changes back the way he'd originally built them and filed a ticket explaining why the customers were wrong. When a third-party API integration came in that he'd never worked with before, he told Maya it wasn't possible before researching whether it was.

She'd hired for yesterday's problems. She'd selected the perfect engineer for a stable, well-specified environment. She worked in a startup. These were not the same environment.

Credentials vs. Capability

The contrast that taught Maya the most wasn't Connor failing. It was watching Alex succeed.

Alex had joined the team with a philosophy degree and a coding bootcamp certificate. He couldn't recite framework internals or discuss algorithm complexity. In Maya's original scoring matrix, he wouldn't have made the first cut. He'd gotten the job because her previous manager had hired him before she'd taken over, and she'd inherited him skeptically.

Alex couldn't tell you how React's reconciliation algorithm worked. He could tell you, within twenty minutes of hearing about a problem, what approach he'd try first, what might go wrong, and what he'd do if it did. He was wrong sometimes. He adjusted and moved on. He asked the team for help without it costing him anything in the telling. He made the people around him better without appearing to try.

Connor had years of experience and a prestigious degree. Alex had less experience and a certificate from a bootcamp. In the environment Maya actually worked in, Alex was twice the engineer.

She ran a postmortem on her own hiring process. The credentials she'd weighted most heavily — prestigious company, recognized school, mastery of the current stack — were predictors of what someone had already done in environments that probably weren't hers. The capabilities she'd underweighted — learning velocity, adaptability under ambiguity, how someone responded to being wrong — were predictors of what they'd do next.

She'd been hiring for a résumé she'd already written. She needed to be hiring for a future she couldn't fully predict.

The Culture Fit Illusion

After Connor, Maya audited her interview questions and found the problem immediately: she'd been testing for cultural vocabulary rather than cultural values.

"How do you handle disagreement with teammates?" Connor had answered this smoothly. He talked about constructive conflict and mutual respect. He'd clearly given this answer before and it had worked before and she'd written "strong" in the notes column.

In practice, Connor's idea of constructive conflict was explaining, at length, why the other person was wrong. His version of mutual respect required the team to respect his technical judgment. He wasn't dishonest in the interview. He genuinely believed he embodied the values he was describing. He just had a different operational definition of each word.

Maya rebuilt the hiring questions around scenarios with specific, awkward details: not "tell me about a time you disagreed with a teammate" but "tell me about a time you were outvoted on a technical decision you thought was wrong, and walk me through what you did next." Not "how do you approach mentoring" but "tell me about someone you worked with who learned more slowly than the rest of the team — what did you actually do?"

The specificity made people uncomfortable in ways that were informative. Candidates who could answer with real examples — including examples where they'd handled it imperfectly — showed something that polished answers never did: actual self-awareness about how they operated versus how they wanted to operate.

The Reference Check Revolution

Maya had been treating reference checks as box-ticking. She'd asked Connor's references generic questions and received generic answers. "Connor is very skilled. Connor produces high-quality work. Connor could be more collaborative." She'd logged the last one as a minor concern and moved on.

That last one had been the whole answer. She just hadn't known how to hear it.

She learned to treat reference conversations as investigative interviews rather than confirmation calls. She stopped asking "how was their performance" and started asking: "tell me about a project that really brought out their strengths — and what kind of project did they tend to struggle with?" "Describe a time when requirements changed significantly midway through. How did they respond?" "If you were staffing a new team and could take two people from your previous org, would they be one of them? Why or why not?"

That last question got silence sometimes. The silence was data.

She also started asking to speak with peers, not just managers. Managers evaluated deliverables. Peers knew how someone actually operated in the weeds — whether they pulled their weight during crunch, whether they gave credit, whether they asked for help or pretended they didn't need it.

The Priya Hire

When Maya hired Priya Nakamura, she applied everything the Connor disaster had cost her.

Priya had less direct experience with their stack than Connor had. She said so freely in the interview, without apology, and immediately described how she'd gotten up to speed on unfamiliar technologies in the past. Maya presented her with a technical problem outside her stated experience to see what she'd do. Priya asked two clarifying questions, said she'd probably approach it this way, flagged where she was guessing, and asked what Maya would do.

Maya almost smiled. That was the move. That was exactly the move.

Priya's references — all three of them, including the peer Maya asked for specifically — described someone who made their teams better. One said: "I would take Priya onto any team I was building. She makes the people around her more rigorous without making them feel inadequate about it. That's rare."

Six months later, Priya had mastered the stack, introduced three improvements to their development practices that the whole team had adopted, and become the person other engineers went to when they were stuck. Not because she was the most experienced. Because she was the most helpful.

Connor had arrived with superior credentials and made the team less capable. Priya had arrived with less experience and made the team more capable. The difference was not the credentials. The difference was the person.

What Sarah Braddock Said About Hiring

Maya told Sarah about the Connor situation on one of their Sunday calls. Sarah listened without interrupting, which was her habit when she was about to say something direct.

"You hired for fit with a job description," Sarah said. "You should have been hiring for fit with the team, the environment, and the next eighteen months — not the last eighteen months."

"How do you tell the difference in an interview?" Maya said.

"You don't, reliably. You improve your odds. You ask about how they've changed their mind on something technical. You watch whether they're curious about your problems or just trying to demonstrate their solutions. You call the reference who seemed reluctant and ask them why. And you accept that hiring is probabilistic, not deterministic. Your job is to improve the odds and learn fast when you got it wrong."

"Connor took four months," Maya said.

"That's actually fast," Sarah said. "Some people take four years to see it."

Before and After

Before: Maya Delacroix hired the way she'd been hired — credentials, technical screen, culture fit question with a smooth answer, reference check that confirmed what she already thought. She selected for people who looked like the job description she'd written, which looked like the problems she already understood.

After: She hired for learning trajectory and collaborative capacity alongside technical skill. Her interviews were uncomfortable in ways she'd deliberately designed. Her reference calls were conversations. She still made mistakes. She made them faster and learned from them sooner.

Replace at least two "tell me about a time" questions with scenario-based questions that require specific, awkward details. "Tell me about a time you were wrong about a technical decision and the team went with it anyway. What did you do?"

Ask to speak with a peer, not just a manager, for at least one reference. Ask the peer: "would you choose to work with this person again, and in what kind of environment would they thrive?"

During the interview, present the candidate with a problem outside their stated expertise and watch the process, not the answer. Curiosity, comfort with uncertainty, and the willingness to say "I'm guessing here" are worth more than a correct solution.

The Priya hire changed the team. The Connor hire almost broke it. One decision, repeated across a career, compounds in both directions.

While Maya was learning to hire for the future, Keisha Williams was dealing with a different challenge entirely: she'd built the most effective operations network in the company, and the matrix restructure had just made it nearly impossible to use.

Chapter 4: Keisha's Communication Revolution - The Art of Modern Communication

For fifteen years at Meridian Manufacturing, Keisha Williams had run operations the way her grandmother ran Sunday dinner: by knowing everything that was happening before it happened, and making sure the right people were in the right place when it did. She read rooms. She caught problems early. She knew which floor supervisor was about to give notice two weeks before he knew it himself.

That was her gift. And when the company restructured into matrix management — product lines crossing departments, dotted-line reporting going every which way — she assumed the gift would travel with her.

It did not travel. Not all of it.

The old network, the one she'd built across fifteen years of hallway conversations and favors given and received, was built for one kind of organization. This new thing, with its cross-functional teams and its shared accountability and its four different bosses needing four different updates in four different formats, that was something else entirely.

She found out just how different during the product launch crisis. In the old structure she would've made three phone calls. In the new structure she needed a communication plan she didn't have. Keisha Williams did not like not having the plan.

The Informal Network Disruption

Keisha's real power at Meridian Manufacturing had never appeared on an org chart. It lived in fifteen years of phone calls returned, favors remembered, problems flagged before they became incidents. She knew which engineering manager to call when manufacturing had a design concern, which logistics director would tell her the truth about a shipment, which VP's assistant was the actual decision-maker for scheduling. That network was the operating system under everything she did.

The matrix restructure didn't eliminate the network. It just made it insufficient.

Suddenly she had dotted-line responsibility across three product lines instead of one. The relationships she'd built were deep in one direction and nonexistent in two others. She could manage her own operation with her eyes closed. She could not coordinate across product lines that had their own cultures, their own priorities, their own informal power structures she hadn't spent fifteen years learning.

The wake-up call came during a product launch crisis. A quality issue in one manufacturing line created cascade effects across two others. In the old structure, three phone calls would have contained it. In the new structure, she needed a cross-functional communication plan she hadn't built and relationships she didn't fully have yet. The crisis resolved. It took longer than it should have, and she knew exactly why.

She sat with that knowledge for a week before she did anything about it. Keisha Williams did not move until she understood what she was moving toward.

The Translation Problem

What Keisha had been doing for fifteen years, without naming it, was translation.

Manufacturing spoke in capacity, throughput, and technical constraint. Logistics spoke in lead time and supplier reliability. Finance spoke in cost per unit and variance from budget. Sales spoke in customer commitments and competitive pressure. None of these languages were wrong. They were the right language for each function's actual work. The problem was that none of them were mutually intelligible without someone in the middle converting.

Keisha had been that someone. She could take a manufacturing floor constraint and explain it to a VP in terms of revenue risk. She could take a customer commitment from sales and walk the logistics team through exactly what it required by Thursday. She'd been doing it so long and so naturally that she'd stopped noticing she was doing it.

The matrix structure tripled the translation burden. Now she was bridging three product lines, each with its own organizational subculture, its own unstated assumptions, its own way of determining who was trustworthy. Her old approach — build the relationship first, establish credibility over time, earn the right to be the translator — was correct but too slow for the scope she now had.

She needed a system for what had previously been instinct. That was not a comfortable realization for someone who had made instinct her competitive advantage.

The Executive Interface Evolution

Before the restructure, Keisha's relationship with senior leadership was clean: she gave operational updates, escalated what needed escalating, implemented what was decided. She was known as someone who delivered without drama. She'd been proud of that.

The matrix structure changed what the executives needed from her. Now she was interfacing with multiple leaders who had different information styles and different definitions of what "updated" meant. One wanted detailed data before any decision. Another wanted a one-paragraph summary and a clear recommendation. A third — and this one took her the longest to calibrate to — didn't want updates at all, just results, and read any proactive communication as a signal that something was wrong.

She made an embarrassing mistake with the third one early on: sent a detailed briefing on a supplier situation that was fully under control, just wanted to keep him informed. He called her two hours later, concerned. She'd accidentally communicated a problem by communicating too thoroughly about its absence.

"Learn your audience," she told her team afterward, which was advice she'd given a hundred times and had just failed to take herself.

The shift that changed her executive relationships: she stopped thinking of those conversations as reporting and started thinking of them as strategic consultation. She wasn't giving updates. She was bringing analysis, options, and a recommendation. That reframe elevated every conversation she had with senior leadership for the next two years.

The Crisis Coordination Test

The supplier quality crisis arrived six months into the matrix structure, which was long enough for Keisha to know she wasn't ready and short enough that she hadn't finished building what she needed.

Components failing across all three product lines simultaneously. Manufacturing, logistics, quality assurance, and sales all needing different information on different timelines. Executives needing confidence that someone was in charge. And Keisha in the middle, coordinating people who didn't all report to her and didn't all trust her yet.

She built a tiered communication structure in real time. Operational teams got hourly updates on the specific information relevant to their function — nothing more, because more would create noise and noise would cost time. Executive leadership got a daily summary with a clear status indicator: contained, progressing, or escalating. Cross-functional leads got a shared channel where decisions were documented the moment they were made.

It worked well enough. Not perfectly — there was a twenty-four-hour gap in the middle where logistics and manufacturing were operating on different assumptions because the channel hadn't been set up yet. She documented that gap and built the missing piece into the standard protocol afterward.

That was Keisha's way: run the thing, find where it breaks, fix the break, update the documentation. She had receipts for all of it.

Influence Without Authority

The matrix structure required something Keisha had never had to develop formally: influence over people who didn't report to her and had no organizational obligation to cooperate.

Her instinct was to rely on the relationships she'd built. That worked with the people she'd known for years. It didn't work with the product line leads she'd met four months ago, who had their own priorities and their own definition of what an operations director from a different line was doing in their business.

What she learned, slowly and through several failed attempts to coordinate things by email: influence in a matrix structure comes from making other people's jobs easier, not from asserting that coordination is important. She started framing every cross-functional request in terms of what the other person's team would gain, not what Meridian needed as a whole. She started showing up to their problems before she needed them to show up to hers.

The breakthrough came with a product line lead named Renata Osei, who'd been visibly skeptical of Keisha's involvement from the start. Keisha noticed that Renata's team was struggling with a supplier onboarding process that Keisha had solved two years earlier for her own line. She offered the documentation and a two-hour walkthrough, no strings. Renata took it.

Six weeks later, Renata was the one pulling Keisha into cross-functional conversations. Not because of obligation. Because Keisha had demonstrated she was useful. That was the currency that worked.

What the Crisis Taught Her

Keisha had a standing meeting with her predecessor — the woman who'd built the operations function before her — every few months over the phone. Retired, lived in Savannah now, still sharp. Keisha called her after the supplier crisis was resolved.

"You're describing what happens to everyone when the job changes shape faster than the skills do," the woman said. Her name was Loretta Fines, and she did not waste words.

"I knew the matrix was coming," Keisha said. "I thought I was prepared."

"Knowing a river is wide doesn't mean you can swim it," Loretta said. "You can't prepare for scale in the abstract. You prepare by building the thing, finding where it breaks, and fixing it. Which is what you did. You're just annoyed it wasn't already built."

Keisha was quiet for a moment. "I am annoyed it wasn't already built," she said.

"Mm-hmm," Loretta said. Which was Alabama for: now you're seeing it clearly.

Before and After

Before: Keisha Williams had spent fifteen years building a network so effective she'd stopped seeing it as a network. It was just how things worked. Then the matrix restructure arrived and the network wasn't enough.

After: She built the scaffolding her instincts had been standing on without her knowing it. Communication tiers. Relationship maps. Protocols that lived in documents, not in her. She was still the best translator in the building. The translation could now happen without her in the room.

Map your informal influence network explicitly — not the org chart, the actual network. Who do you call when something is about to go wrong? Who calls you? Where are the gaps in people you should know but don't?

For each executive stakeholder, identify their information preference: do they want data or summary, updates or results, options or recommendations? Calibrate accordingly and watch what changes.

Find one cross-functional relationship that's transactional and make it substantive. Show up to their problem before you need them to show up to yours. Loretta Fines would call this farming. Keisha calls it the only kind of influence that actually lasts.

Keisha's communication revolution was about expanding the reach of what she already did well. David's next chapter is about something harder: discovering that the hands-off style he'd been proud of was actually leaving one of his best people behind — so gradually that he almost missed it entirely.

Chapter 5: David's Performance Puzzle - Performance Management That Works

David was proud of how hands-off he was. He said this — actually said it out loud — to new hires during onboarding: "I believe in hiring great people and trusting them." He thought this was enlightened management. He thought this was what good bosses did.

What he was actually doing, he understood later, was avoiding the uncomfortable parts of his job.

Cameron had been on the team for four years. Good designer, steady output, no drama. David would've described him as solid, reliable, one of his best — and he would've meant it, right up until the moment he realized Cameron had been quietly declining for eight months without David catching it once.

The work was still technically adequate. That was the tell he'd missed. Cameron didn't miss deadlines. He didn't create problems. He just gradually stopped doing the thing that had made him excellent, and David, who was busy trusting his great people, never noticed until the client did.

"I thought I was giving him room to breathe," David said later. "Turns out I was just not paying attention. Those are two different things."

The Output vs. Performance Distinction

Cameron Reyes had been on David's creative team for four years. Senior designer, reliable, no drama. David would have described him as one of his best, and he would have meant it sincerely, right up until the moment a client pulled David aside after a campaign presentation and said, quietly, that the work felt like it was on autopilot.

David went back through the last eight months of Cameron's deliverables. On time, every one. Technically sound, every one. And reading them in sequence, he could see exactly what the client meant: Cameron had been doing correct work. He had not been doing inspired work. At some point in the last year, the spark had gone out, and the output had continued — adequate, punctual, uninspiring — and David had been tracking the output, not the performance.

Those are different things. Output is what someone produces. Performance is the quality of thinking behind it, the engagement that generates it, the trajectory it's on. Cameron's output had been fine. His performance had been declining for eight months. David hadn't seen it because he'd been measuring the wrong thing.

"I realized I'd been managing Cameron's deliverables," David said, rubbing the back of his neck. "I missed the person making them. That's on me, mano."

The Gradual Decline Problem

The reason David missed it for eight months wasn't negligence. It was the nature of gradual decline: it doesn't look like a problem until it does, and by then it's been a problem for a long time.

Cameron wasn't missing deadlines. He wasn't creating conflict. He wasn't doing anything that would have triggered David's intervention instincts. He was succeeding just enough to stay invisible while slowly becoming less than he'd been.

David also had four years of Cameron's goodwill sitting in his mental ledger. When a piece came in that felt flat, he'd unconsciously attributed it to a bad week rather than a pattern. That attribution felt generous. It was actually lazy. He'd been giving Cameron the benefit of a doubt he hadn't earned recently, based on a reputation earned years ago.

What he needed was a way to track trajectory, not just current state. He started keeping brief weekly notes on each team member — not a formal system, just observations. The quality of thinking in a piece, not just whether it shipped. Whether someone's contributions to a brainstorm had changed in tone or ambition over the last month. Whether a person seemed to be operating from curiosity or from habit.

Within six weeks of starting that practice, he could see two other early-stage versions of what had happened with Cameron. He caught them early enough to do something about it. That was the difference.

Capability vs. Effort: The Diagnosis That Changes Everything

David's first instinct when someone's performance dropped was to assume motivation. They'd stopped trying. They needed to recommit. He'd have a talk with them about standards and expectations.

With Cameron he tried that and it went nowhere. Cameron was not unmotivated. He came in on time, worked the hours, cared about the quality of his craft. Telling him to try harder was the wrong prescription for the wrong diagnosis.

What Cameron actually lacked was strategic context. For four years he'd been executing other people's concepts. He'd never been asked to contribute at the conceptual level, so he hadn't developed the muscle for it, and as Meridian's clients got more sophisticated and started expecting that kind of contribution from senior designers, Cameron was delivering at a level that no longer matched what senior meant.

The fix wasn't motivation. It was development. David connected Cameron with a design strategist at a partner firm for a six-week mentorship. He started including Cameron in the early-stage briefings where conceptual framing happened, instead of handing him work that was already shaped. He gave Cameron one project with real creative latitude and stayed out of it.

Six months later the client who'd flagged the autopilot problem called David to say that Cameron's recent work on their account was the best thing they'd seen from Meridian in years. David forwarded the email to Cameron with no comment. He didn't need to add anything.

Individual vs. Systemic: Knowing the Difference

The post-restructuring slump wasn't Cameron's problem alone. When David looked honestly at the team after the client departure, he saw variations of the same pattern: people who'd been excellent in a stable environment showing signs of drift in an unstable one.

His first instinct was to address each person individually. He caught himself before he did that, because he'd learned from Cameron that individual conversations about systemic problems produce individual explanations that miss the actual cause.

The systemic problem was that the team had lost its largest source of creative ambition. The client that had departed wasn't just revenue — it had been the account that pushed Meridian to do its best work. Without that pressure, the team had been operating in a lower gear without realizing it.

David brought that diagnosis to Carla rather than treating it as a team morale issue. She helped him make the case for a new-business initiative that would bring in accounts with the same creative ambition as the one they'd lost. It took four months. It worked. The team's output improved before the new client even started, because the expectation of challenge changes how people work.

That was the systemic fix. The individual conversations still happened. But they happened after he'd addressed the environment, not instead of it.

The Difficult Conversation He'd Been Avoiding

David had been putting off the direct conversation with Cameron for two months before he finally had it. He knew why: he liked Cameron, Cameron liked him, and the conversation was going to be uncomfortable in a way that threatened that.

He had it anyway, because Cameron deserved it and because David had finally understood that avoiding difficult conversations wasn't kindness, it was selfishness dressed as consideration.

He opened it differently than he would have six months earlier. Not: here's what I've observed and here's what needs to change. Instead: "I've been watching your last eight months of work and I think something's shifted. I'd like to understand it from your side before I tell you what I'm seeing."

Cameron talked for twenty minutes. Felt disconnected from the strategic direction of client projects. Wasn't sure where to contribute at the level that was being asked of him. Had been covering that uncertainty with technical execution because execution was safe.

David recognized the feeling immediately. It was exactly what he'd experienced during the restructuring crisis: uncertainty covered by activity. He told Cameron that. Cameron looked at him for a moment and said: "I didn't think you saw any of that."

"I didn't," David said. "For too long. That's why we're talking now."

What Carla Told Him About Performance

David brought the Cameron situation to Carla at a point when he thought he'd already solved it. He was wrong.

"You fixed one person," Carla said. "What's the system that would have caught it earlier?"

He didn't have a good answer. He had the weekly observation notes, which were new. He didn't have a formal performance framework, didn't have differentiated expectations by career level, hadn't defined what excellent looked like at senior versus mid level in a way he'd actually communicated.

"Performance management is not the annual review," Carla said. "The annual review is a summary of whether you did your job during the year. Performance management is the ongoing practice of knowing whether people are growing, stuck, or declining — and doing something about it before it shows up in a client call."

David built the framework over the next quarter. Not complicated — he'd learned his lesson about complicated. Clear expectations by level. A quarterly conversation about trajectory with every team member, separate from the project check-ins. A rubric for what "excellent" meant at each stage so people knew what they were aiming at.

It was the management infrastructure he'd never built during the five years of winging it. He was building it now, problem by problem, one hard conversation at a time.

Before and After

Before: David Rodriguez managed output. Deadlines hit, quality adequate, no visible drama — that was good enough. He was generous with praise and conflict-averse about everything else. His team liked him. They also, without his knowing it, had learned not to expect much from him when they were struggling quietly.

After: He managed performance. That meant tracking trajectory, not just delivery. It meant diagnosing capability gaps rather than assuming motivation problems. It meant having the uncomfortable conversation two months earlier than was comfortable, because Cameron deserved a manager who noticed. The team still liked him. They also, now, trusted that he was paying attention.

Your Performance Assessment Actions

Start keeping brief weekly observations on each team member — not a formal system, just notes. Quality of thinking, not just output. Are they operating from curiosity or from habit? Do this for sixty days and see what patterns you couldn't see before.

The next time you're about to address a performance issue, stop and diagnose first: is this a capability gap, an effort problem, or a systemic issue? The fix for each one is completely different. Treating them the same way is the most common performance management mistake.

Schedule one conversation this month that you've been putting off because it's uncomfortable. Open it by asking what they're experiencing before you say anything about what you've observed. The order matters more than you think.

Cameron recovered. He's still at Meridian. That outcome required David to catch something he almost missed entirely, and to have a conversation he'd been finding reasons to delay.

Maya had just finished rebuilding her team after the Connor disaster and thought she'd figured out the hiring problem. Then she hired Brett Callahan. Different name, same dynamic, except this time it wasn't just one difficult person — it was a team chemistry collapse that took her three months to understand and another three to fix.

Chapter 6: Maya's Team Chemistry - Reading People and Building Trust

Eight months in, Maya had finally stabilized the team. She had communication protocols that worked, delegation frameworks that were actually getting used, one-on-ones that didn't feel like dentist appointments anymore. She had data on all of it.

Then she hired Brett Callahan.

His credentials were legitimate. His references checked out. He answered every technical question correctly. In the debrief after his final interview, every person on the panel said some version of "seems solid." Including Maya. She was measuring the wrong things, again, and this time she knew enough to recognize it afterward but not enough to catch it in time.

Within two weeks Brett had reorganized the team's informal communication patterns in ways Maya was still untangling three months later. He hadn't done anything she could write up. He'd just introduced a subtle tax on collaboration — a raised eyebrow here, a comment in code review there — and the team had started going quiet in exactly the ways teams go quiet before they fall apart.

"Twelve pages," Maya told her mentor Sarah, meaning: she'd already started a document logging what was wrong and still hadn't let herself say it out loud. "Apparently credentials are a terrible proxy for judgment." She'd already opened a document and started logging observations. Twelve pages before she let herself admit what she already knew.

The Invisible Team Chemistry Patterns

Brett Callahan's first week looked fine. His second week looked fine. By his third week, Maya's team was subtly different in ways she couldn't immediately name.

The brainstorming sessions got quieter. Not silent — quiet. People were still contributing, but the half-formed ideas, the wild pitches, the "what if we tried" experiments that Nora and Alex had been generating freely for months had tapered off. The Slack channel where the team shared interesting problems and possible approaches had slowed to near-zero.

Brett wasn't doing anything obviously wrong. He wasn't rude. He wasn't hostile. He was technically excellent and he knew it, and when someone shared an incomplete idea, he would evaluate it and explain, clearly and at length, why it wouldn't work. He was usually right. The ideas usually didn't work yet — that's what half-formed means. The team had been generating half-formed ideas freely because that's how they'd built the good ones. Brett had introduced a tax on that process without intending to, and the team had quietly stopped paying it.

"I hired someone who was perfect on paper," Maya told Sarah Braddock. "There is apparently a very large gap between paper and actual." She'd already started a document. Twelve pages of observations before she let herself say what she already knew.

Reading the Room: What Maya Learned to See

The Brett situation forced Maya to build what she'd been missing: a systematic way to observe how her team actually operated, not just what they produced.

She started watching the same things in every team interaction. Who spoke first in meetings and who waited. Who asked questions and who gave answers. When someone's code review comments changed in tone. Whether people were making eye contact in video calls or looking slightly off to the side in the way people do when they've already checked out. Whether the ratio of questions to statements in one-on-ones had shifted.

None of these were conclusive on their own. In combination, over time, they told her things that her output metrics never would. Nora had stopped asking clarifying questions in team reviews — which meant she'd either gotten much more confident or had stopped caring, and Maya could tell from the rest of the signal which one it was. Alex had started front-loading his contributions at the beginning of meetings and going quiet afterward, which was new, and the timing corresponded exactly with Brett's arrival.

She developed what she called a people-reading practice: not a framework with a name, just a habit of watching how people changed relative to themselves over time. Not compared to each other. Compared to who they'd been.

The practice didn't tell her what to do. It told her what was happening early enough to do something about it.

The Cultural Integration Attempt

Maya tried to integrate Brett for two months before she admitted to herself that integration wasn't the right word for what was needed.

She paired him with Alex on projects. She gave him explicit feedback about how his code review style was landing. She created structured brainstorming formats designed to make it easier for half-formed ideas to be shared without immediate evaluation. Brett adapted his behavior slightly in each case — enough to seem responsive, not enough to change the underlying dynamic.

The problem wasn't that Brett was refusing to adapt. The problem was that his default operating mode — independent, evaluative, certain — was incompatible with how this team needed to function. You couldn't manage someone into a fundamentally different personality. You could coach behavior at the margins. You couldn't coach values.

She brought it to Sarah Braddock on a Sunday call. Sarah asked: "What are you waiting for?"

Maya said: "I'm waiting to be sure."

Sarah said: "You have twelve pages of observations. You've tried three different interventions. You're not waiting to be sure. You're waiting until it's bad enough that the decision is obvious, so you don't have to own it."

That was an uncomfortable sentence. It was also accurate.

Trust Rebuilding After the Damage

By the time Maya made the personnel decision, the team had been operating in a lower gear for three months. The brainstorming culture hadn't recovered on its own. Trust doesn't revert to baseline when the source of damage is removed — it has to be actively rebuilt, and the rebuilding takes longer than the damage did.

She started with transparency, which was not her default. She told the team directly that she'd seen what had happened, that she'd waited too long to act, and that she took responsibility for the months of diminished collaboration. She did not ask them to validate her decision or reassure her that she'd done the right thing. She just named what had happened and said she was sorry it had taken as long as it did.

Nora was the first to respond. She said: "I didn't think you noticed."

Maya said: "I noticed late. That's different from not noticing, but it's still too late."

That conversation — the willingness to own the mistake without explaining it away — did more for team trust than the personnel decision itself. People don't need their manager to be perfect. They need to know their manager is honest about being imperfect. The team started generating half-formed ideas again within two weeks of that conversation. Maya tracked it in her notes like a vital sign.

The Personnel Decision Framework

The Brett situation gave Maya something she'd needed since the moment she became a manager: a framework for personnel decisions that didn't rely on waiting until the situation was obviously untenable.

Three questions. First: is this person willing and able to adapt to how this team needs to function? Not in theory, based on their stated intentions. In practice, based on observable behavior change over a defined period. Second: what is the cost to the rest of the team of continuing to invest in the integration? This cost is almost always underestimated because it's distributed across many people and hard to quantify. Third: am I waiting because I genuinely believe change is coming, or because the decision is uncomfortable?

The third question is the one she runs first now. Because if the honest answer is the second option, the other two don't matter yet. She needs to deal with her own avoidance before she can think clearly about the situation.

She'd learned that protecting team culture was a management responsibility, not an HR one. If she was the only one who could see the chemistry problem and she didn't act on it, no one would. The team had trusted her to see it. She'd seen it late. She wouldn't make that mistake at the same speed again.

What the Brett Situation Taught Her

Technical competence is necessary and insufficient. She already knew this from Connor. Brett confirmed that she'd learned the lesson intellectually but hadn't built it into her hiring and evaluation process deeply enough to catch a more sophisticated version of the same problem.

Team chemistry is fragile and asymmetric: hard to build, easy to damage, slow to restore. One person operating at odds with the collaborative norms of a team can degrade a culture that took a year to build in a matter of weeks. Managers who wait until the damage is obvious have already waited too long.

And the most important thing: the conversation Maya had been avoiding was not the personnel decision. It was the honest conversation with herself about why she was avoiding it.

Before and After

Before: Maya Delacroix managed individuals and tracked their output. She noticed team dynamics when they broke down visibly. She addressed personnel problems when they became impossible to ignore.

After: She managed the team as a system with its own health indicators. She watched how people changed relative to themselves over time. She built a framework for personnel decisions that forced her to name her own avoidance before she could assess the situation clearly. She still made the decisions later than she should have. She made them earlier than she used to.

Your Team Chemistry Diagnostic

Pick one person on your team and track one behavioral indicator — not output, behavior — over the next thirty days. How often do they volunteer ideas in group settings? Do they ask questions or only give answers? Does their communication style change under deadline pressure? One person, one indicator, thirty days. See what you learn.

If there's someone on your team whose impact on team dynamics you've been explaining away, run the three questions: willing and able to adapt in practice? Cost to the team of continued investment? And — most importantly — are you waiting because you believe change is coming or because the decision is uncomfortable?

The answer to the third question tells you everything about what to do next.

While Maya was rebuilding her team's collaborative culture, Keisha Williams had taken her first real vacation in two years. By day three, her phone had forty-seven messages. By day five, she was answering emails from a beach in Tybee Island about a process question that was right there in her own documentation. She flew home early. That trip was the

beginning of a much harder realization about what she'd built
and what she'd failed to build.

54

Chapter 7: Keisha's Knowledge Vault - Building Systems That Survive

The vacation was supposed to be ten days. Eleven with travel.

By day three, her phone had forty-seven messages. By day four, Marcus on the floor had made a supplier decision she would never have made and couldn't reverse. By day five, she was sitting on a beach in Tybee Island answering emails about a process question that was right there in the documentation — her documentation, the documentation she'd written — and her team could not find it without her because they had never been asked to look.

She flew home early. Told her husband it was urgent. He didn't argue because he'd been watching this happen for years.

"You made yourself the system," he said that night. She didn't answer him. He was right, and being right about something Keisha Williams had already identified as a problem did not require a response.

The Institutional Knowledge Trap

The forty-seven messages were waiting when Keisha checked her phone on day three in Tybee Island. She'd told herself she wouldn't check until day five. She lasted until after breakfast on day three.

Fourteen of them required a decision that only she could make. Eight were questions about processes she'd documented, which meant people couldn't find the documentation or didn't trust it without her confirmation. Six were Marcus Oduya keeping her informed of things he'd decided, not asking permission, but clearly not sure he'd decided correctly. The rest were updates she'd asked to be copied on before the vacation and now regretted asking for.

She answered what couldn't wait and put her phone down. Her husband watched her from his beach chair. He did not say anything. They had been married long enough that silence was a full sentence.

She flew home on day five. Told him it was urgent. He helped her pack. On the drive to the airport he said: "You built a machine and then made yourself the only part that couldn't be replaced." She said: "I know." He said: "I've known for two years." She did not respond to that, because there was nothing to say that wasn't just a variation of: you're right and I didn't want to see it.

The Knowledge Documentation Framework

The first thing Keisha did when she got back was pull up the process documentation and read it as if she were a new employee who had never met her.

It was not usable. She could see that immediately. It described what to do in standard situations. It did not describe how to decide what situation you were in. It listed the steps for supplier escalation without explaining the judgment calls embedded in each step — the ones Keisha made automatically, from fifteen years of knowing which supplier would respond to urgency and which one needed to be approached differently. The documentation was a transcript of her actions. It was not a transfer of her thinking.

She rebuilt it in three layers. The first layer: explicit procedures for routine operations, usable by anyone with basic training. The second layer: decision trees for complex but predictable situations, with the judgment criteria written out rather than assumed. The third layer: principles for genuinely ambiguous situations — not rules, because rules don't work when the situation doesn't match the rule, but the underlying reasoning that produced the rules, so someone could work from first principles when the playbook ran out.

The third layer was the hardest to write because it required Keisha to articulate things she'd been doing on instinct for so long she'd stopped knowing she was doing them. She spent three weeks on it. She had her team read drafts and tell her where they still had to guess. Every place they had to guess was a place the documentation had failed.

Distributing Decision Authority

The documentation problem was solvable. The authority problem was harder, because it wasn't really an authority problem. It was a confidence problem that Keisha had accidentally created.

For years, when her team had flagged an issue, she'd resolved it. Quickly, correctly, without drama. Her team had learned, reasonably, that Keisha was the path of least resistance for any decision with real consequences. They'd stopped building the muscle for those decisions because Keisha had been exercising it for them.

She couldn't fix this by announcing that people should make more decisions. You don't build capability through declaration. She fixed it by withdrawing — deliberately, with warning — from decisions she'd been making that her team should be making.

She told Marcus directly: "For the next ninety days, I want you to make the call on any supplier decision under fifty thousand dollars. Don't check with me first. Tell me what you decided and why after the fact. I'm going to let you be wrong sometimes. That's part of it."

Marcus was quiet for a moment. "What if I make a bad call?"

"Then we'll fix it and you'll make a better one next time," Keisha said. "A bad call you learn from is worth more than a good call I make for you."

He made three calls she would have made differently in the first month. None of them were disasters. One of them was actually better than what she would have done, which she told him, because that was the truth and the truth mattered more than her ego.

The Relationship Transfer Challenge

The hardest knowledge to transfer wasn't process knowledge. It was relationship knowledge.

Keisha's supplier relationships were built on trust that had accrued over years of her being reliable, reasonable, and straight with people. When she said there was a problem, suppliers believed her. When she said something could wait, they waited. That credibility wasn't transferable by introduction. It had to be earned separately by the person inheriting the relationship.

She started bringing her team members into supplier conversations not as observers but as participants. Not: "this is Marcus, he'll sometimes be in touch." But: "Marcus is the person to talk to about capacity planning — he's been working on this for six months and he understands the constraints better than I do at this point." The second framing transferred some of her credibility while also being true. Marcus did understand the capacity planning. She'd made sure of it.

She also created relationship maps — not just names and contact information but context: what each supplier cared about, what their constraints were, what history mattered, what had gone wrong before and how it had been resolved. The kind of thing that lived in her head and died with her departure if she didn't write it down.

It was tedious work. She did it anyway, because she understood something that she wished she'd understood five years earlier: if the knowledge only lives in one person, it's not organizational knowledge. It's a liability.

Testing Whether the System Actually Worked

Three months after she'd started rebuilding, Keisha took another vacation. Eight days this time, same destination. She left her laptop at home.

She checked her phone on day four — not because anything required it, out of habit. Eleven messages. Three were updates Marcus had sent because he thought she'd want to know, not because he needed her. Two were from Loretta Fines, who didn't know Keisha was on vacation and was just keeping in touch. The rest were things that could wait until she returned and did.

She put her phone back in her bag and went back to the beach.

Her husband didn't say anything. He didn't need to. Some things you demonstrate rather than announce.

When she returned, she debriefed with Marcus on what had happened while she was gone. One decision she would have made differently. She asked him to walk her through his reasoning, not to correct it, but to understand it. His reasoning was sound. The difference was experience, not judgment. Experience was the part that came with time. Judgment was what she'd been building.

What Loretta Fines Told Her

Keisha had told Loretta about the vacation crisis on one of their calls. Loretta had listened without commenting, which was her version of taking it seriously.

"You made yourself the single point of failure," Loretta said finally. "Every good manager does this at some point. The ones who stay good catch it."

"I caught it late," Keisha said.

"You caught it. That's the part that matters. Now answer me this: if you left tomorrow, what would break?"

Keisha ran the list. It was shorter than it would have been six months ago. It was not as short as it needed to be.

"That's your list," Loretta said. "Work the list. Not because you're leaving. Because an organization that depends on one person to function isn't an organization. It's a person with staff."

Keisha wrote that down. She put it in the third layer of her documentation, under principles.

Before and After

Before: Keisha Williams was the best operations manager Meridian had ever had, and the organization's single point of failure. Both of those things were true. She'd built something excellent and made it irreplaceable, which is not the same as sustainable.

After: The knowledge lived in systems. Marcus Oduya made decisions she used to make, and made some of them better. The supplier relationships had been transferred rather than just inherited. If Keisha left tomorrow, things would be harder. They would not stop.

Your Knowledge Transfer System

Pull up your most important process documentation and read it as if you've never met yourself. Where does someone still have to guess? Every gap is a failure of transfer, not a failure of the reader.

Identify one decision type you've been making yourself that someone on your team should be making. Tell them directly, with the parameters, and then let them be wrong once in a controlled way. The learning from that wrong call is worth more than your clean decision record.

Ask yourself Loretta's question: if you left tomorrow, what would break? Work the list. Not because you're leaving. Because the answer tells you exactly where the organization is still depending on you rather than on the systems you've built.

Keisha spent the next eighteen months working her list. David Rodriguez, meanwhile, had just acquired a new boss who was systematically dismantling his authority in public, and was about to discover that keeping your head down only works when

the person above you isn't actively using your head as a
footstool.

Chapter 8: David's Politics Problem - Managing Up and Across

David had always believed in keeping his head down and doing good work. This belief had served him well for most of his career, and then it completely failed him the moment Victoria Brennan became his boss.

Victoria had a style David had never encountered outside of a management case study: high expectations, low context, and a talent for making decisions in meetings David wasn't invited to and holding him accountable for them afterward. She was not incompetent. That was the frustrating part. Her strategic thinking was sharp. She just had no interest in David's opinion and a way of making that clear in front of other people.

Six months in, he was second-guessing decisions he'd been making confidently for years. His team could feel it. Zoe asked him in a check-in if everything was okay and he said yes — too fast, which is how she knew it wasn't.

He called his abuelo that weekend. The old man listened for a while and then said: "Mijo, a bad boss is like a bad referee. You don't get to argue the calls. You learn to play around them."

David wasn't sure that was useful advice. He wrote it down anyway.

The Authority Erosion

Victoria Brennan had been David's boss for three months when she overrode a project timeline he'd presented to the full creative team. Not in private, where he could have absorbed it and moved on. In front of his team, mid-meeting, without asking a single question about how he'd arrived at the estimate.

She wasn't wrong that the timeline was aggressive. She was also not right in a way that justified the override. It was a judgment call, and she'd made it in the room in a way that made clear whose judgment counted.

David kept his expression neutral the way he'd learned to when the Cowboys were losing in the fourth quarter. He finished the meeting, walked to his office, closed the door, and sat very still for two minutes.

Victoria wasn't incompetent. That was the frustrating part. Her strategic thinking was sharp. Her industry knowledge was real. She had a track record of transforming agencies. She also had a management style that treated public override as a valid tool for establishing authority, which was effective for establishing authority and catastrophic for the people underneath her.

By month six, David was second-guessing decisions he'd been making confidently for years. His team could feel it. Zoe pulled him aside after a briefing and said: "David. Are you okay?" He said yes, too fast. She nodded slowly in the way that meant: I heard your answer and I don't believe it.

The Preemptive Influence Strategy

David's first instinct had been to prove himself through the work. Victoria would see the results, see that his judgment was sound, and adjust. That strategy failed completely because Victoria wasn't updating on evidence. She was operating from a prior about what kind of manager David was, and she'd formed it in the first month.

He changed strategies. He stopped trying to demonstrate his judgment after the fact and started trying to shape her thinking before she made decisions.

He studied her patterns. She made decisions faster when she'd been briefed in advance and slower when she was encountering something cold. She responded better to quantitative framing for creative decisions than to qualitative arguments, even when the qualitative arguments were stronger. She was more receptive to new approaches on Tuesdays and Wednesdays and more defensive on Fridays, when she was already thinking about what she'd need to defend to her own leadership over the weekend.

He started sending pre-briefs before any decision he cared about. Two paragraphs, clean structure, the data front-loaded. He framed his proposals in terms of what Victoria could present upward rather than what he thought was right. He presented options rather than recommendations, because Victoria was more likely to choose something she felt she'd selected than something she felt she'd been told to do.

It worked often enough to be worth doing. It was also exhausting in a way he hadn't anticipated. He was spending significant mental energy managing one relationship upward when that energy had previously gone to the team. He logged this cost carefully. He wasn't sure yet whether the math worked out.

The Information Problem

The deeper frustration was that Victoria made decisions based on context David didn't have. She'd override something he'd built carefully and cite "strategic priorities" or "executive alignment" without explaining what those meant in practical terms. He was being held accountable for decisions made in rooms he wasn't invited to.

He started attending the optional leadership meetings he'd previously skipped. He started building relationships with Victoria's peers — the other department heads — not to go around her but to understand the organizational context that was shaping her decisions. When he understood that Victoria was under significant pressure from the CEO to demonstrate measurable ROI on creative investment within two quarters, her behavior became less arbitrary and more legible. He still didn't like it. He could work with legible.

He also started keeping a brief log of decisions that had been made without his input and then attributed to his responsibility. Not a complaint document — a factual record, dated, with the relevant context. His abuelo had taught him: document everything you might need and hope you never need it. The restaurant business had made the old man cautious in ways that were occasionally useful.

The Credit and Blame Navigation

The pattern that wore on David most wasn't the overrides. It was the credit distribution.

When the GlobalTech campaign performed above projections, Victoria presented it to the executive team as a product of the new strategic direction she'd brought. When a mid-tier client expressed concerns about responsiveness, Victoria described it in her summary as a team execution issue. Both characterizations were simplified to the point of being misleading. Neither was a lie David could easily refute without looking like he was fighting for credit, which was its own kind of bad look.

He got deliberate about visibility. He started cc'ing Carla — his previous department head, who was still in the organization — on client communications that represented significant wins. He volunteered for a cross-functional initiative that put him in direct contact with two members of the executive team. He started contributing to the agency's newsletter with brief pieces about the creative team's work, published under his name with Meridian's communications team's approval.

None of this was aggressive. All of it was deliberate. He was building a presence in the organization that didn't entirely depend on Victoria's narrative about him. It was work he should have been doing for years. Victoria had just made the cost of not doing it visible.

Building Alliances

David had always thought of alliance-building as the kind of political maneuvering that people with bad intentions did. He updated this belief during month seven of working for Victoria.

Alliances, he came to understand, are just relationships with people who have organizational influence and understand your work. He'd had those relationships before Victoria arrived. He'd just maintained them casually, as friendships, rather than deliberately, as a professional network. The difference mattered when things got hard.

He invested in three relationships specifically: Carla, who knew his track record and had credibility with senior leadership. The creative director at a sister agency who could speak to his industry standing. And the GlobalTech account lead on the client side, who could validate the quality of Meridian's creative output in terms that carried independent weight.

He didn't mobilize any of them against Victoria. He cultivated them because a career built on one person's opinion of you is one bad boss away from collapse. He was learning that lesson at significant personal cost, and he intended to learn it completely.

What His Abuelo Told Him

David called his abuelo on a Saturday morning when the Victoria situation had been going on for four months and he was tired of carrying it alone.

He explained the dynamic. The abuelo listened, the way he always listened, without interrupting and without showing what he thought until David had finished.

"At the restaurant," his abuelo said, "I had a landlord for twelve years who was a difficult man. Raised the rent when he could, delayed repairs when he could, found reasons to make things harder than they needed to be."

"What did you do?" David said.

"I built the best restaurant I could, I kept every record he might ever dispute, and I built relationships with everyone else in the building so that my reputation didn't depend on what he said about me." The old man paused. "And when I finally had the leverage to move, I moved. You don't fight a bad landlord. You outlast them or you leave."

David sat with that for a while. "I'm not sure I'm ready to leave," he said.

"Then you're in the outlasting phase," his abuelo said. "Do it with dignity. That's the whole strategy."

Before and After

Before: David Rodriguez believed that good work spoke for itself and that office politics were for people who couldn't deliver results. He'd spent five years building a team and zero years building the organizational presence that would protect that team when his boss became a problem.

After: He managed up deliberately, not reactively. He kept records. He built relationships that existed independently of his reporting line. He framed his work in terms of what his organization's leadership needed to hear, not just what was true. He was still the person who bought tacos and remembered people's kids' names. He was also, now, someone who couldn't be easily written out of his own story.

Your Difficult Boss Navigation Toolkit

Study your boss's decision-making patterns for thirty days before you try to influence anything. When do they move fast versus slow? What kind of framing makes them more receptive? What context are they operating in that you don't have visibility into? Understand before you act.

Build organizational relationships that don't route through your boss. Not to undermine them — to ensure your professional reputation isn't entirely dependent on their account of your work. Do this before you need it.

Keep a factual record of significant decisions: what was decided, who made the call, what the outcome was. Hope you never need it. Keep it anyway.

David outlasted Victoria. She was moved to a different role eighteen months after she arrived. He was still at Meridian when she left. He'd also, in those eighteen months, built capabilities he wouldn't have developed in a comfortable reporting relationship. There are worse ways to be educated.

Maya's education was about to arrive in the form of an all-hands email on a Tuesday morning that began with the phrase "transformative partnership" and ended with the word "acquisition." She had forty-eight hours to figure out what that meant for her team before Sterling Financial's integration team arrived to start figuring it out for her.

Chapter 9: Maya's Change Challenge - Leading Through Change

The acquisition email came on a Tuesday at 8:47 AM. Maya read it twice — once for content, once for implication — and then opened a new spreadsheet.

Sterling Financial was acquiring FinTechFlow. The CEO called it a "transformative partnership." Maya had been in enough meetings to know what corporate language meant when it was working that hard. She started a tab labeled "retention risk" and began typing names.

Eighteen months she'd been Engineering Team Lead. She'd built something she was proud of — not just the code, though the code was solid, but the team. The way they worked together. The trust. Nora presenting confidently now in the meetings she used to go quiet in. Marcus making architecture decisions without needing Maya's sign-off every time. That had taken months.

Sterling wouldn't see any of that. Sterling would see a spreadsheet with roles and salaries and redundancies. Maya called her mom that night. Her mother asked in Creole if she was eating and if her team was okay, in that order. Maya said yes to both, which was partially true, then filed the worry away in the part of her brain where she kept things she'd deal with when she had more data.

The Survival Economics Reality

Maya read the acquisition email twice before she opened a spreadsheet. The first read was for content. The second was for implication. The spreadsheet was for the thing she didn't want to think about yet: which of her eight engineers was Sterling Financial going to decide they didn't need.

She labeled the tab "retention risk" and started typing names.

She knew what "transformative partnership" and "optimization opportunities" meant in corporate language. She'd been in enough all-hands meetings to have decoded the vocabulary. She gave herself forty-eight hours before Sterling's integration team arrived, and she spent those forty-eight hours building the best possible case for every person on her team.

The survival economics were cold and she understood them without flinching: Sterling had bought FinTechFlow for its payment processing technology, not its engineering culture. The technology would be evaluated. The team would be evaluated on whether they were necessary to maintain and improve the technology, or whether Sterling's existing engineers could absorb the work. Her job for the next three months was to make the answer to that question obvious and favorable.

She called her mother that night. Her mother asked, in Creole, if she was eating and if her team was going to be okay, in that order. Maya said yes to both, which was partially true. She filed the worry in the part of her brain where she kept things she'd deal with when she had more data. The spreadsheet had seventeen rows. She went back to it after the call.

The Layoff Participation

Three months into the integration, Sterling's HR lead asked Maya to participate in the personnel evaluation process for her own team. They framed it as "leverage her institutional knowledge." What they meant was: help us decide who to cut, and make sure the process is defensible.

She understood immediately what was being asked and what would happen to her if she refused. Managers who refused to participate in personnel evaluations during acquisitions were themselves evaluated as resistant to integration. She had seen it happen at companies she'd heard about secondhand. She was now seeing the mechanics of it up close.

She participated. She did it carefully, which meant understanding the legal requirements around documentation and non-discrimination before she said anything in any meeting. She made sure the criteria were job-relevant and consistently applied. She advocated for the people she could advocate for on business grounds and was honest about the people she couldn't.

The hardest conversation was with Nora. Not because Nora was at risk — she wasn't; her skills were genuinely rare — but because Nora came to Maya directly and asked: "Are we going to be okay?" Maya could not lie to her. She also couldn't tell her everything she knew. She said: "I'm fighting for everyone. I can't promise outcomes I don't control." Nora held her gaze for a moment and nodded. It was not a satisfied answer. It was an honest one, and Nora was smart enough to know the difference.

Three engineers were let go. Maya had not been able to save them. She had been able to ensure they left with full severance, positive references, and a personal introduction to two companies she'd identified as likely fits. That was the limit of what was in her power. She sat with the limit for a long time before she accepted it.

The Technology Consolidation Politics

Sterling's engineers had their own infrastructure, their own architectural preferences, and a strong organizational incentive to demonstrate that FinTechFlow's technology was valuable in ways that required FinTechFlow's engineers specifically to maintain. Both of those things were true simultaneously and in tension with each other.

When Sterling's architecture team proposed replacing FinTechFlow's payment processing core with Sterling's existing system, Maya recognized the proposal for what it was: a technically plausible recommendation that was also a political move to establish Sterling's engineering team as the primary organization.

She prepared her counter not as a technical argument but as a business case. FinTechFlow's processing core handled edge cases in the regulatory compliance layer that Sterling's system didn't cover, and those edge cases were specifically relevant to three of Sterling's existing clients who were currently processing around the gaps manually. The cost of the manual workarounds was significant and had been attributed to a different line item in a way that had made it invisible.

She presented this in a meeting with Sterling's CTO, calmly, with numbers. The replacement proposal was tabled. She didn't treat it as a victory. She treated it as one data point in a longer negotiation about where FinTechFlow's technology fit in Sterling's future.

She'd learned something from the Alex meeting two years ago: lead with what the other person needs to know, not with what you need them to believe.

The Cultural Assimilation Demand

Sterling expected FinTechFlow's remaining engineers to adopt their culture, their processes, and their communication style immediately. This was not negotiable. Acquisitions that allowed the acquired company to maintain a distinct culture created two-tier organizations, and Sterling's leadership had seen that go badly before and had strong opinions about preventing it.

Maya understood the organizational logic. She also understood that "adopt the culture immediately" meant "absorb several years of organizational norms in ninety days," which was the kind of instruction that was impossible to follow and would be held against her team if they fell short.

She became the translator. She learned Sterling's internal vocabulary, their meeting formats, their reporting structures, and their unstated expectations. She briefed her team not with "here's how to comply" but with "here's how they think about things, and here's what that means for how we operate." She framed the cultural shift not as submission but as bilingualism. Her team had been code-switching in technical contexts for years. This was the same skill applied organizationally.

She also adapted her own communication style to Sterling's norms faster than her team did, which gave her credibility with Sterling's leadership and political room to give her team more time to adjust. She was the bridge. She'd been the bridge her whole career.

Strategic Positioning Under Pressure

The question Maya returned to consistently during the integration: what does this team do that Sterling cannot easily replicate?

The answer changed as she learned more about Sterling's engineering organization. The processing core was part of it — she'd already made that case. The regulatory compliance expertise was another part, because FinTechFlow had spent three years building domain knowledge that Sterling's team had not needed until the acquisition. And the team's speed — their ability to move from specification to deployment in timelines that Sterling's more mature organization couldn't match — was a capability that had not yet been demonstrated inside Sterling's infrastructure but could be.

She built the case systematically and presented it in pieces over the first four months, each time connecting FinTechFlow's capabilities to Sterling's stated strategic priorities. She had learned from watching Victoria: the framing that works is always the one that shows the other person getting what they want.

By month six, her team had been assigned two of Sterling's highest-priority infrastructure projects. That was the outcome she'd been building toward from the Tuesday morning of the announcement.

What Sarah Braddock Told Her About Surviving Acquisitions

Maya called Sarah on a Sunday, later in the acquisition than she should have. She'd been handling it herself for three months and was tired in a way that wasn't about sleep.

"You're managing the politics correctly," Sarah said, after Maya had talked for twenty minutes. "You're not managing the team's emotional experience of it."

"I don't have time for that right now," Maya said.

"I know that's what it feels like," Sarah said. "Here's what's true: your team is scared and they're watching you to calibrate how scared to be. You're managing them by not managing them, and they're filling the uncertainty with their worst-case assumptions. That is costing you more than you think."

Maya scheduled a team meeting for the following Tuesday. Not a status update. A conversation about how the integration was going for each person, what they were finding hard, what they needed from her. She had not created an agenda. She let it be what it was.

Nora said she felt like a guest in a building she didn't understand yet. Alex said he missed knowing who he was in the organization. Marcus said he was fine and then, five minutes later, said he was actually not fine and explained why.

Maya listened without problem-solving. People-first, problem-second. The sticky note was still on her monitor. She looked at it during the meeting without meaning to.

Before and After

Before: Maya Delacroix had built a team she was proud of and an organization that valued them. An acquisition arrived and neither of those things protected her engineers from being evaluated as a line item.

After: She'd learned to read organizational power, translate between corporate cultures, and make the case for her team in terms the acquiring company could hear. Three engineers still lost their jobs. The other five came through knowing their manager had fought for them. That distinction matters.

Your Crisis Leadership Preparation

If your company were acquired tomorrow, what is the irreplaceable case for your team? Not the general case — the specific capabilities, domain knowledge, or speed advantages that would be difficult for the acquiring organization to replicate. Build that case now, before you need it.

When your team is under uncertainty, schedule a conversation that isn't about the work. Ask how they're experiencing the situation. Don't problem-solve. The information you get will be more useful than any status update.

Learn the acquiring organization's vocabulary and priorities before you try to advocate for anything. The framing that lands is always the one that shows them getting what they want.

Maya's team came through the acquisition intact, with two of Sterling's highest-priority projects. Five people went through something that could have been worse and came out knowing their manager had fought for them. That mattered as much as the project assignments.

David was about to face a different kind of multiplication problem. Meridian had just landed the biggest contract in the agency's history, which should have been a celebration and was instead the beginning of six months that nearly broke him.

Chapter 10: David's Growth Gambit - Scaling Teams and Systems

In David's personal cosmology, the ideal team was six to eight people — tight enough that everyone knew when someone was having a bad week, flexible enough to turn on a dime. Small. Smart. Fast. He'd said this to anyone who asked, which in retrospect was probably the universe preparing him to be proven wrong.

GlobalTech's contract would require doubling his team in six months. Then doubling again.

He found out on a Monday and spent the rest of the week with the feeling he got when the Cowboys made the playoffs — like something good was definitely about to go wrong in a way he couldn't predict but could absolutely sense.

He was right about the feeling and wrong about nearly every tactical decision he made in response to it. He hired too fast, onboarded too slowly, and worked three consecutive eighteen-hour days trying to compensate for a structural problem that longer hours could not fix.

His wife sat him down on a Saturday morning and said: just list what's breaking. He listed nine things. She said, which three actually matter? He stared at the list for a long time. It was the first useful management thought he'd had in six weeks, and it hadn't been his.

The Contract That Changed Everything

GlobalTech's five-year, fifty-million-dollar marketing contract was the biggest thing that had ever happened to Meridian, and David Rodriguez spent the first weekend after signing it with a low-grade dread he couldn't explain to anyone who asked how he felt.

He knew how he felt. He felt like the Cowboys had made the playoffs. Which meant something good was definitely about to go wrong in a way he could sense but not prevent.

The contract required doubling his team of twelve in eighteen months. The performance penalties for missed deadlines or quality failures were real money — not symbolic, not embarrassing, genuinely consequential for Meridian's financial position. He had never managed under those conditions. He had never managed more than fifteen people. He was about to do both simultaneously.

"I thought scaling meant growing gradually and learning as you go," he told his wife, working through the third eighteen-hour day in a row. She said: "What actually happened?" He said: "It turns out you just have to build the plane while flying it and the plane has to land in six months or the airline loses a million dollars." She told him to go to sleep. He did not go to sleep.

The Talent Acquisition Problem

The creative talent market was competitive in a way David had not experienced before. He was trying to hire eight senior designers and writers in a market where every boutique agency with a big client had the same idea. He was competing on speed and Meridian couldn't always win on compensation.

He made hiring decisions faster than he was comfortable with and accepted compromises he wouldn't have accepted in a slower environment. Three of his first five hires were good. One was fine. One was a problem he identified in week two and had to manage out by month three, which cost him time he didn't have and created instability in a team that was already operating at the edge of its capacity.

The cascade effect of one bad hire under pressure is worse than it is in a stable environment, because every person a bad hire affects is also under pressure, and pressure reduces tolerance for exactly the kind of friction a bad hire generates. David learned this at some cost and built a faster assessment process for his next round of hiring: a focused two-stage interview that prioritized stress tolerance and speed of adaptation over portfolio depth. Imperfect. Better than what he'd had.

Quality Under Velocity

GlobalTech's brand standards were more rigorous than anything Meridian had worked with before. New team members were learning those standards at the same time they were producing work to those standards, which was a quality assurance problem that David's existing review process couldn't absorb.

He built a tiered review system he was not proud of but that worked: a fast internal check for brand compliance on every deliverable, a slower quality review for anything going to the client, and a weekly calibration meeting where the team looked at a sample of recent work against the standard together. The calibration meeting was the piece that mattered most — it turned quality assessment from a manager function into a team function, which meant the standard lived in the team's working memory rather than in David's approval queue.

He still had to kill work sometimes. It was never comfortable. He got faster at it. "This doesn't meet the standard" is a complete sentence, and he'd spent five years softening it into something longer and less clear. Under GlobalTech's timeline, he didn't have room for that anymore.

The Financial Reality

David had managed project budgets before. He had not managed a contract that represented forty percent of his company's revenue with performance penalties embedded in the structure.

He found out the hard way that he didn't fully understand his own cost model. The revenue projections Meridian had built for GlobalTech assumed productivity levels that his expanded team hadn't reached yet and wouldn't reach for another four months, because new hires aren't immediately productive at the level of experienced hires and he'd known this abstractly without building it into his assumptions.

Carla caught it in the third-month financial review. She did not make him feel good about having missed it. She also helped him build a realistic revised model and present it to the CFO before it became a larger problem. That was the managing up lesson applied: bring the problem with the analysis rather than hoping the problem resolves itself.

He went back to the taco principle afterward, because he needed to understand it completely to stop using it. The taco principle wasn't just about management style. It was about resource allocation. He'd been spending relationship currency on appreciation instead of on the harder work of communicating accurate expectations upward. GlobalTech was correcting that.

The Leadership Capacity Limit

Month four was when David hit the wall he hadn't believed was there.

He'd scaled the team. He'd built the review process. He'd fixed the cost model. And he was running on insufficient sleep, seeing everything through the filter of exhaustion, and making decisions that were fast and slightly worse than decisions he'd been making six months earlier. His team could feel it. Zoe mentioned it to him directly, which she wouldn't have done if it weren't visible.

The actual problem: he'd scaled the headcount without scaling the leadership structure. He was still trying to manage twenty-four people the way he'd managed twelve — with personal relationships, direct involvement, his own judgment applied to individual decisions. That model had a person-capacity limit, and he'd exceeded it.

He promoted Zoe to creative lead and gave her explicit authority over the design team's work. He hired a senior writer to lead the content team. He moved himself out of day-to-day project decisions and into a role that was more about strategy, client relationship, and the team leads' development. He hated giving up the direct involvement. He did it anyway, because the alternative was continuing to make slightly-worse decisions while being tired and pretending that was acceptable.

His abuelo had said: you don't scale a restaurant by working longer hours. You scale it by building a kitchen that runs without you in it. David had taken four months to apply advice he'd heard at the age of twelve.

What Carla Told Him About Hypergrowth

"You made the classic mistake," Carla said, in her direct way, during a check-in at month five. "You optimized for the thing you could see, which was headcount, and underbuilt the thing you couldn't see, which was leadership infrastructure."

"I built a review process," David said.

"You built a quality process. That's different from leadership infrastructure. Leadership infrastructure is the thing that makes decisions without you. You're still the decision-maker for everything above a certain threshold and that threshold is too low."

David asked what the threshold should be. Carla said: "Low enough that you're occasionally surprised by decisions that got made correctly without you. Right now you're never surprised because nothing gets decided without you. That's the signal that you're still the bottleneck."

He moved the threshold. He was surprised twice in the next month by good decisions his team leads had made without him. He told them both, explicitly, that the decision had been right. That was the management work: not making the calls, but making clear what a good call looked like when his team made one.

Before and After

Before: David Rodriguez believed the ideal team was six to eight people, tight and fast. He managed through personal relationship and direct involvement in most decisions. That model worked at one scale and failed completely at another.

After: He'd built a leadership structure that could function without him in every decision. He'd learned to hire under pressure with a faster and imperfect process that was still better than no process. He'd moved from being the decision-maker to being the person who built decision-makers. He still thought the ideal team was probably six to eight people. He was now also capable of running a team of twenty-four, which was a different and harder skill.

Your Hypergrowth Readiness Assessment

If your team doubled in size next quarter, what would break first? Not the work — the management structure. Where are you the bottleneck? What decisions currently route through you that don't need to? Build the answer to that question before the growth happens.

Your cost model for a growing team needs to account for the productivity ramp of new hires. New people are not immediately equivalent to experienced people on headcount. If your projections don't account for that, your financials will correct you on a timeline that won't be comfortable.

The signal that you've successfully delegated authority is being occasionally surprised by a decision that got made correctly without you. If you're never surprised, you're still the bottleneck.

GlobalTech became the contract that made Meridian. It also came close to breaking David before it made him. He'd come through it with capabilities he wouldn't have built in a comfortable environment.

Keisha was about to find out that building something excellent doesn't guarantee it survives you. She'd spent four years creating one of the best operations organizations in the company. Six months after her promotion, she was getting reports that her successor was dismantling it, piece by piece, for reasons that made complete sense from his perspective and none from hers.

Chapter 11: Keisha's Institutional Impact - When Good Work Gets Undone

Keisha knew the transition was going to be complicated. She'd done everything right — documented her processes, cross-trained Marcus Oduya, spent six months making sure he understood not just what she did but why. She'd been thorough. She'd been deliberate. She told herself she'd built something that would last.

Six months after the promotion, her former colleagues started sending carefully worded messages. The kind people write when they're not sure if they're allowed to say what they want to say. Reading between the lines, which Keisha had done her whole career: the supplier partnership program was being restructured. The cross-functional coordination protocols were being "simplified."

Marcus wasn't dismantling her work out of malice. She understood that. He'd come up in a different kind of organization, with different priorities, different metrics. He was making reasonable decisions by his own logic.

That was what stung. Not that he was wrong exactly. Just that four years of her work had lasted about six months past her departure. Her grandmother would've said: "Baby, you built a house, not a foundation." Keisha had been sitting with that all week.

The Sustainability Illusion

The reports from her former colleagues started arriving six weeks after Keisha's promotion. Carefully worded messages, the kind people write when they're not sure they're allowed to say what they want to say. Reading between the lines, which Keisha had done her whole career: the supplier partnership program was being restructured. The cross-functional coordination protocols were being "simplified." The documentation she'd built, the three-layer framework she'd spent months on, was being described by Marcus's team as "too complex for day-to-day use."

She sat with the reports for a week before she called anyone. That was her way: understand before you react.

What she understood after a week: she had built programs that were excellent and had not built the institutional scaffolding that would sustain them without her. The supplier partnerships had delivered real savings. They had also required her specific relationships, her specific judgment about when to press and when to wait, and her specific authority with the vendors who had learned to trust her over years. Marcus hadn't dismantled her work out of incompetence. He'd encountered the parts that depended on Keisha and had replaced them with something that didn't.

"I thought I was building something that would outlast me," she told her husband. He was quiet for a moment. "You were building something excellent," he said. "That's not the same thing."

Understanding Marcus

Keisha drove to Birmingham the following month to spend a weekend with her grandmother, who was eighty-one and still sharp in the way of people who have spent a lifetime paying attention.

Keisha described the Marcus situation. Her grandmother listened, then said: "So he's doing what makes sense for his job, and you're upset because it's not what made sense for yours."

"My approach produced better outcomes," Keisha said.

"For your context. With your relationships. Under your priorities." Her grandmother poured more sweet tea. "Baby, you didn't build him a house. You gave him a house you'd been living in for fifteen years and expected him to keep it decorated the same way."

Keisha thought about that for the rest of the weekend.

Marcus wasn't wrong by his own logic. He'd come up in a more process-standardized organization and believed in standardization as a value. The supplier partnership approach — relationship-intensive, judgment-dependent, contextual — looked like organizational risk to him because it was. It worked because of Keisha. He didn't have Keisha. He standardized it.

She could not be angry at him for making a reasonable decision with the resources he actually had. She could be honest with herself about what she'd failed to transfer.

The Value Communication Failure

The part that stung most: the programs Keisha was proudest of were her preventive work. The supplier disruptions that hadn't happened. The quality failures that had been caught early. The coordination failures that had been avoided because she'd been watching for them.

Preventive value is invisible to people who haven't experienced the problems being prevented. Marcus hadn't been at Meridian before Keisha's programs existed. He had no reference point for what those programs had prevented. To him, the programs were overhead. The outcomes they produced were just the baseline.

She had not built the documentation to make preventive value visible. She'd documented what to do, not what had been prevented by doing it and what would happen if it stopped. That was the failure. Not that the programs were discontinued, but that she'd left the case for them entirely in her own institutional memory, which left with her.

She started keeping a different kind of record in her new role: not just what the operations produced, but what problems were not occurring because of how the operations were structured. She tracked near-misses. She documented the decisions that had prevented them. She wrote the counterfactual explicitly: without this protocol, this would have happened. She would not make the same mistake twice.

The Institutional Embedding Framework

The question Keisha returned to consistently: what would have made the programs survive?

Not better documentation alone — Marcus's team had read it and called it too complex. Not better relationships with Marcus alone — she'd tried to transfer those and they'd partially taken hold but not deeply enough. The answer she arrived at over several months of thinking: the programs needed to be embedded in organizational structures that existed independently of her.

Structural embedding meant: the supplier partnership methodology needed to appear in job descriptions, in performance metrics, in budget allocations. Not as a program Keisha ran, but as an organizational capability that the operations role was accountable for delivering. If it was in the job description, the next person in the role inherited the obligation, not just the option.

Coalition embedding meant: the people who benefited from the programs needed to be visible advocates, not just satisfied recipients. The logistics directors and product line leads who had benefited from the supplier partnerships needed to be on record saying so, to leadership, in terms that connected to business outcomes. When Keisha was the only person making the case for a program, the program depended on Keisha's presence. When five other leaders were making the case, the program had a coalition.

She rebuilt her programs in her new role with both layers from the start. It took longer. They lasted.

Building the Coalition

The coalition work was the part Keisha found most uncomfortable, because it required asking people to advocate for her programs publicly, which felt like asking for something.

She had spent her career being valuable without asking for credit. This was different.

Loretta Fines, as usual, cut through it. "You're not asking for credit," she said. "You're building the organizational memory that the program works. Those are different activities."

Keisha started having different conversations with the stakeholders who benefited from her programs. Not: do you appreciate what we're doing? But: would you be willing to speak to this in the quarterly review? The answer was usually yes, because the programs were genuinely producing value and people were willing to say so when asked directly.

She also started connecting the programs explicitly to strategic priorities in her own communications upward. Not: here's what operations is doing. But: here's how what operations is doing connects to the competitive positioning you described in Q3. That framing made the programs harder to cut because cutting them became visible as cutting something strategically relevant.

Her grandmother had said: build a foundation, not a house. Keisha was building foundations.

What Loretta Told Her About Lasting Impact

"Everything you build will be modified by whoever comes after you," Loretta said, on one of their calls. "The question isn't whether they'll change it. They will. The question is whether the underlying value survives the changes."

"How do you make sure it does?" Keisha said.

"You build the value into the organization's identity, not just its processes. When an organization believes that a certain capability is part of who it is, leaders defend it because abandoning it feels like abandoning something essential. When it's just a process, leaders change it because processes are supposed to be changeable."

Keisha thought about that. "That's a different kind of work than what I've been doing."

"Mm-hmm," Loretta said. "Longer horizon. Less visible. More lasting."

Keisha started working the longer horizon.

Before and After

Before: Keisha Williams built programs that were excellent. They were also entirely personal — held together by her judgment, her relationships, her presence. When she left, what remained was a set of procedures the next person couldn't fully use.

After: She built programs designed to outlast her. Structural embedding. Coalition support. Counterfactual documentation. The programs were designed for a successor she hadn't met yet, with priorities she couldn't predict. Most of them survived. That was the point.

Your Institutional Impact Framework

For your most important initiative, ask: what would a competent successor with different priorities do with this? If the honest answer is "dismantle it," ask what would have to be true for them not to. Work toward that.

Document the counterfactual, not just the outcome. What problems is this program preventing? What would happen if it stopped? Make that case explicitly, in writing, before you leave the role.

Build your coalition before you need it. The stakeholders who benefit from your work should be on record saying so. Ask them directly. It is not the same as asking for credit.

Keisha's programs at Sterling Financial outlasted her. That took different work than building the programs themselves. It took thinking about succession from the first day, not the last.

Maya's acquisition integration was complete. She'd come out the other side as Engineering Director, responsible for decisions that would affect FinTechFlow's competitive position for years. The next chapter is about what senior technical leadership actually requires, which turned out to be significantly different from what she'd expected even after everything she'd already learned.

Chapter 12: Maya's Management Mastery - From Technical Leader to People Developer

Maya Delacroix spent her first weekend as Engineering Director building a model of FinTechFlow's entire engineering organization — capabilities by team, dependencies, technical debt by system, key-person risk by name. Forty-three variables.

The model told her things she already half-knew: the payment processing core was held together by two engineers being actively recruited by larger companies. The mobile team was eighteen months behind where it needed to be. Technical debt in the legacy API layer was compounding at a rate that would become a serious problem in about fourteen months if nobody addressed it.

She presented this to the CEO on a Wednesday. He looked at it for a long time and then said: "What's your recommendation?"

She had one. She always had one. The question was whether she could translate it — from technical precision into business logic into the executive narrative he thought in. That translation problem was the new job. She'd been code-switching her whole life, between Creole and English, between engineer and manager. This was one more language to learn.

"When I was a team lead, my biggest decision was which engineer to assign to which project," she told her mentor Sarah. "Now I'm making choices that will determine whether this company exists in five years. Nobody warned me the jump was that large."

The Decision That Changed the Frame

The microservices question sat on Maya's desk for three weeks before she answered it. Not because she didn't know the technical answer — she did, she'd known it within forty-eight hours of the promotion — but because the technical answer wasn't the answer she was being asked for.

The CEO needed to know whether to commit eighteen months and three million dollars to a fundamental infrastructure change during a period when FinTechFlow was trying to demonstrate value to Sterling Financial and maintain competitive positioning in a market moving faster than it had two years ago. That was a business decision with technical inputs, not a technical decision with business implications. Maya had spent two years learning the difference between those two things without knowing she was learning it.

She presented her recommendation on a Wednesday. The CEO asked three questions, all of them business questions. She answered all three with data she had prepared specifically because she'd anticipated he would ask them. He approved the project.

She walked back to her office and sat down and thought: that was the job. Not the two hours of whiteboarding with the engineering team. Not the architecture diagram. The three questions and the prepared answers. The translation. She'd been translating her whole life. Now she was doing it at a level where the stakes were different.

The Engineering Talent War

Within six months of the promotion, Maya had lost two engineers to companies offering equity packages she couldn't match. Both were people she'd developed. Both were good. She was not surprised by either departure and was still not fully prepared for either one.

The retention problem at director level was different from the retention problem at team lead level. At team lead level, retention is about the immediate work environment — the team, the manager, the quality of the projects. At director level, retention is about trajectory. Senior engineers stay where they believe they're building something that will matter and where they can see what their career looks like in three years.

She started having different conversations with her senior engineers. Not: here's what you're working on. But: here's where the technology is going, here's where I see your expertise fitting into that future, here's what I'm building toward and why I need you specifically in it. She was selling a future, not a job. Most people stay for futures they believe in.

She still lost people. Less often. The ones who left were easier to plan for because she'd had the trajectory conversations and knew which engineers were satisfied with where they were headed and which ones were restless. Restless engineers on a timeline are easier to manage than restless engineers you didn't know were leaving until they told you.

The Board Communication Problem

Maya's first board presentation was, by her own assessment, technically accurate and strategically useless.

She had prepared it the way she'd prepared technical briefings: comprehensive, precise, organized by system component. The board members, who were investors and executives and one former regulator, had no context for most of what she'd presented and no clear answer to the question they were actually asking, which was: is our engineering investment generating competitive advantage, and do we have the right person leading it?

Sarah Braddock talked her through it afterward. "You answered questions they didn't ask," Sarah said. "They asked two questions. Are we winning technically? And can we trust you to tell us if we're not? You presented a system architecture instead."

"The system architecture is the answer," Maya said.

"It's the evidence. The answer is yes or no, followed by why, followed by what you're doing about it. Board members allocate capital. They need to know where to allocate it and whether the person asking for it understands the business well enough to be trusted with it. Lead with that."

The second board presentation was seven slides. The first slide was a one-sentence answer to each of their two questions. The remaining slides were the evidence. The board asked four questions during the presentation, all of which she answered without going back to the slides. That was when she knew the preparation had been right.

Building the Engineering Culture

The team Maya inherited as director was good. It was also fragmented — three subteams that had developed distinct working styles and an informal hierarchy that didn't match the org chart. The payment processing team thought of themselves as the core team and the others as supporting functions. This wasn't stated. It was expressed in a hundred small ways that added up to a cultural problem that would compound as the organization scaled.

She didn't address it with a culture initiative. She addressed it with a structural decision: she reorganized two projects to require genuine cross-team collaboration on work that mattered, where the outcome depended on all three teams performing well together. If you want people to act like one team, give them a problem that requires them to be one team. The culture follows the work.

She also made the engineering values explicit in a way that previous leadership hadn't. Not a values statement on a wall. A set of specific behaviors she named and modeled and referenced in real situations. What it looked like to raise a quality concern before shipping. What it looked like to ask for help rather than spin on a problem alone. What it looked like to disagree with a technical decision through the right channel rather than around it. Specific, behavioral, observable. She'd learned from the Brett situation that naming values doesn't work. Naming behaviors does.

The Industry Platform

A conference invitation arrived in month eight: a fintech security panel at an industry conference, asking if Maya would speak about payment processing architecture.

She almost declined. She was busy, the topic was sensitive given Sterling's acquisition, and she wasn't sure what she had to say that other people weren't already saying.

Sarah Braddock told her to go. "Your reputation is an organizational asset, not just a personal one," she said. "When you're visible in the industry, your company benefits from your credibility. When you're invisible, you're dependent on other people's accounts of your work. You've spent enough time being dependent on other people's accounts of your work."

Maya went. She spoke for twenty minutes about regulatory compliance architecture in payment processing and took questions for ten. Three people came up afterward with business cards. One of them was a senior engineering leader at a company she'd been trying to build a partnership with for six months. He'd heard her talk and wanted to meet.

She started saying yes to the invitations. Not all of them — she was still running an engineering organization and the work came first. But enough of them that she was visible in the industry, which meant FinTechFlow was visible, which had value that showed up in recruiting, in partnerships, and in the Sterling board meetings where her credibility was occasionally relevant.

What Sarah Braddock Told Her About Senior Leadership

"The trap at your level," Sarah said, "is thinking that getting promoted to director means you've arrived. You haven't arrived. You've been assigned a different set of problems that you don't have the instincts for yet because you haven't done this before."

"What are the instincts I'm missing?" Maya said.

"Thinking in organizational time rather than project time. Project time is quarters. Organizational time is years. The architecture decision you're making now should be evaluated by what it enables three years from now, not whether it solves this quarter's problem. You're good at thinking in project time. You're still developing the longer view."

"How do you develop it?"

"You make decisions with a three-year frame and see how they land. You'll be wrong sometimes. You adjust. The instinct comes from practice, not from understanding the concept." She paused. "Also: find people who have done this longer than you and pay attention to how they think, not just what they decide. You're good at the what. You need the how."

Maya wrote that down. She started attending the executive leadership forums she'd been skipping because they weren't directly relevant to her engineering work. They weren't directly relevant to her engineering work. They were directly relevant to her development as a director, which was starting to feel like a different job than engineering director.

Before and After

Before: Maya Delacroix was a very good engineering team lead who had been promoted to director and was running the director role with team lead instincts. She was doing the work correctly and framing it wrong, preparing presentations accurately and missing what the audience actually needed, building good technical culture and not yet connecting it to organizational strategy.

After: She'd developed the translation layer between engineering excellence and business outcomes that director-level technical leadership requires. Her board presentations landed. Her retention conversations were strategic rather than reactive. Her culture decisions were structural rather than aspirational. She was still learning. The problems were harder and more interesting than the ones she'd had as a team lead. That was the sign she was in the right place.

Your Senior Technical Leadership Development

For your next major technical decision, build the business case alongside the technical recommendation. Not instead of it — alongside it. The audience for the decision may be technical. The decision itself is organizational.

Have trajectory conversations with your senior contributors: where they see their career going, what they're trying to build, whether what you're building together connects to that. Do this before they're restless. Do it when things are good, so you know what you're actually working with.

Start saying yes to the industry invitations. Your reputation is an organizational asset. Being visible in your field benefits your team and your company, not just your resume.

Maya's path from team lead to Engineering Director took two years and an acquisition and a set of problems she couldn't have anticipated. She wouldn't trade any of it, which is not the same as saying it was easy.

David was about to have his worst week in four years of management. Everything went wrong simultaneously, and the five fires didn't add up — they compounded. That's the next chapter. It's not comfortable reading. It's useful.

Chapter 13: David's Perfect Storm - Crisis Management Under Fire

Four years. David kept coming back to that number the week everything collapsed. Four years of building something, and it took approximately five business days to threaten all of it.

Monday: GlobalTech called an emergency meeting. "Fundamental concerns with creative direction." David had been in marketing long enough to know that phrase was two steps from "we're going with someone else." Tuesday: his lead copywriter announced she was taking a position at a competitor. She'd been recruited for months. He hadn't known. He should have known.

Wednesday through Friday: a harassment complaint, a potential discrimination lawsuit from a contractor, and a directive from senior leadership to cut his team budget fifteen percent while also somehow recovering the GlobalTech account.

He called his abuelo on Friday night. The old man was quiet for a while and then said: "How many fires?" "Five," David said. "You got a system for that?" "No." "Well," his abuelo said, "now you're going to build one." He wasn't wrong. He was, as always, not wrong in the most unhelpful possible way.

"I spent four years learning to manage one problem at a time," David told his wife after the worst week of his career. "Nobody taught me what to do when five disasters hit at once and two of them are probably your fault."

The Week Everything Compounded

Monday: GlobalTech called an emergency meeting. "Fundamental concerns with creative direction and project execution." David had been in marketing long enough to know that phrase was two steps from termination notice. He took the call from his car so his team wouldn't see his face.

Tuesday: his lead copywriter announced she was taking a position at a competitor. She'd been recruited for four months. He hadn't known. He should have known — he'd had the trajectory conversation with her eight months ago and she'd seemed engaged, and he'd logged that and moved on and hadn't checked back. That was a failure of follow-through and he knew it while she was still in his office.

Wednesday: a harassment complaint against one of his senior designers, filed by a junior team member who had been on his team for six weeks. He had not seen it coming. He was not sure if that meant it hadn't been visible or that he hadn't been looking.

Thursday: a potential discrimination complaint from a contractor whose engagement hadn't been renewed. The contractor's attorney had sent a letter. David read it three times before he called HR.

Friday: Meridian's CFO sent a directive to cut the creative team's budget by fifteen percent while simultaneously recovering the GlobalTech relationship.

He called his abuelo Friday night. "How many fires?" the old man said. "Five," David said. His abuelo was quiet for a moment. "You got a system for five fires?" "No." "Well," his abuelo said, "now you're going to build one."

The Triage Framework

The first thing David did wrong was try to address all five crises simultaneously by working longer hours. He was running on five hours of sleep by Wednesday of the following week, making decisions slightly worse than his normal decisions, and creating new problems through the errors in his tired ones.

He stopped and did what his crisis management instinct had always been too scattered to do: he sorted.

The harassment complaint required same-day engagement regardless of everything else. It had legal implications, human implications, and the potential to compound if he delayed. He handed himself over to HR and let them lead the process, which felt like losing control and was actually the right move. He was not the right person to manage a harassment investigation. HR was.

The discrimination complaint required his documentation, his attorney, and not much else from him in the immediate term. He provided the documentation, briefed the attorney, and stepped back. This crisis had a timeline measured in weeks, not days.

The GlobalTech relationship was the business-critical crisis. He called the account lead directly — not through the agency's formal channel, person to person — and asked for a meeting with no agenda other than to understand what had gone wrong from their perspective. That conversation was harder and more useful than anything else he did that week.

The copywriter departure and the budget cut were real problems that could not be addressed until the first three were stabilized. He made peace with that. Some problems have to wait. Making peace with what has to wait is a skill he hadn't known he was missing.

The Crisis Interaction Effect

The individual crises were manageable. The compounding was the problem.

The GlobalTech concern had partly developed because his lead copywriter had been managing the account's content relationship, and her disengagement during the months she was being recruited had degraded the quality of that relationship without David noticing. Two crises, one root. The harassment situation created a climate of anxiety on the team that affected the quality of work going to GlobalTech during the exact weeks when GlobalTech's trust was already fragile. Two crises compounding into a third.

David had been treating each crisis as separate because they had arrived separately. They weren't separate. They were a system of failures that had developed in parallel and were now interacting. Understanding that didn't make the crises easier. It made the sequencing clearer: address the things that were making the other things worse first, even if they weren't individually the most urgent.

He stabilized the team's internal climate first — a brief, honest team meeting that acknowledged the situation without sharing confidential details. Not a pep talk, not a panic. Just: this is a hard week, here's what I'm focused on, here's what I need from you, ask me directly if you have questions I'm able to answer. The meeting took twenty minutes. The anxiety in the team dropped noticeably afterward. Climate affects output. He'd known this and had still underweighted it.

Managing Stakeholders Through the Fire

David had four stakeholder groups who needed different things from him simultaneously: GlobalTech, his team, Meridian's senior leadership, and the individuals involved in the legal situations.

He mapped what each one needed and what he could and couldn't tell them. GlobalTech needed to know the issues had been identified and corrective action was underway. His team needed to know he was in control of something, even if not everything. Senior leadership needed honest assessment plus a recovery plan, not a reassurance that everything was fine. The legal situations required his full cooperation and very few words not approved by the attorney.

He prepared specific communications for each group rather than improvising. Improvised crisis communication tends toward two failure modes: over-disclosure, which creates new problems, and under-disclosure, which creates distrust. Prepared communication gave him the right amount of information for each audience.

The GlobalTech call was the most important. He had thirty minutes with their CMO. He spent twenty of them listening. He did not defend the work that had disappointed them. He asked what excellent would have looked like. He took notes. He said: I'm going to come back to you in two weeks with a plan for getting there. He did. GlobalTech stayed.

The Team Performance Question

The hardest judgment call of the week: how much to ask of his team while they were stressed and he was managing crises that affected their colleagues.

He got it wrong in both directions. On Tuesday he pushed the team to hit a GlobalTech deadline at a quality level that was below what they were capable of and that he knew was below what they were capable of and that he let through anyway because the alternative was missing the deadline. The client noticed. That cost him trust he didn't have to spare.

On Thursday he pulled the team off a deadline because he thought they needed recovery time, and the deadline was actually more recoverable than he'd assessed. He'd overcorrected.

The lesson he took from both: during a crisis, decisions about team capacity need to be made with the team, not for them. Not every decision — he was still the manager. But capacity assessments benefit from the input of the people whose capacity is being assessed. He'd been deciding from the outside. The outside view was incomplete.

What Carla Told Him Afterward

David debriefed with Carla three weeks after the crisis week, when the legal situations were in the hands of the people whose job it was to handle them and GlobalTech had signed a modified statement of work.

"You handled the triage correctly eventually," Carla said. "You wasted about four days before you stopped trying to do everything simultaneously."

"I know," David said.

"The other thing: you had no early warning system for any of this. The copywriter situation had been developing for months. The team dynamic that produced the harassment situation had been visible to people who weren't you. The GlobalTech relationship had been degrading in ways your account review process should have caught." She paused. "You built minimum viable infrastructure for normal operations. You need minimum viable early warning for things that go wrong slowly."

David sat with that. He'd built the decision framework, the quality review, the leadership structure. He'd built them to manage the work. He hadn't built anything to detect the early stages of the things that nearly sank him.

He built the early warning system over the following quarter. Quarterly retention conversations with everyone, not just the people he was worried about. A monthly account health review that tracked relationship quality, not just deliverables. A standing item in his team leads' check-ins: what's developing that I don't know about yet? That last question, asked consistently, surfaced three situations in the next six months that would have become crises if he'd found out later.

Before and After

Before: David Rodriguez had decent instincts, a good team, and no early warning system for anything that developed slowly. When five crises hit the same week, he had no triage framework and no way to see the compounding until it was already happening.

After: He had both. The triage framework was simple: legal first, business-critical second, important-but-not-urgent third, everything else waits. The early warning system was simpler: one standing question in every team lead check-in. What's developing that I don't know about yet? Three situations surfaced in the next six months that would have become crises. They didn't.

Your Crisis Management Preparation

Build your triage framework before you need it. For any crisis: what requires legal or HR engagement immediately? What is business-critical? What is important but can wait forty-eight hours? Sorting correctly at the start saves significant time and energy over the course of a multi-crisis week.

Add one early warning question to your regular check-ins with team leads: what's developing that I don't know about yet? Ask it consistently. The answers will surface situations when they're still manageable.

When multiple crises compound, address the thing that is making the other things worse first, even if it isn't individually the most urgent. Understand the system of failures before you prioritize the individual elements.

David's worst week became, eventually, the thing that built his best management infrastructure. That's not a silver lining. It's just what happens when you survive something and pay attention to why.

Three years after the crisis week, Maya, David, and Keisha had each arrived somewhere they couldn't have described from where they'd started. The last chapter is about what mastery actually looks like from the inside — which is not what most people expect.

Chapter 14: The Leadership Trajectory - What Mastery Means

Three years is enough time to know whether a lesson actually stuck.

David Rodriguez knew because he'd built Rodriguez Creative from the rubble of the GlobalTech crisis and it was, by any measure, working — twelve people, three flagship clients, systems that held under pressure. The crises still came. They no longer felt like the end of the world. They felt like problems, which was different.

Maya Delacroix knew because she was sitting in a Federal Reserve advisory meeting explaining fintech security architecture to people who made policy, and nobody in that room doubted she belonged there. She'd stopped counting the times she was the only Black woman, the only person under thirty-five, the only engineer. She filed those observations and moved on. There was work to do.

Keisha Williams knew because the operational framework she'd rebuilt — the one designed this time to survive her departure, properly embedded, with real coalition support — was being implemented across nine Sterling Financial facilities. She'd learned from what happened with Marcus. She didn't particularly enjoy that she'd had to.

What Mastery Actually Looks Like

David Rodriguez's first reaction when someone called him a seasoned manager was to laugh. His second reaction was to remember the five-fire week and the taco principle and the four months of winging it that preceded his first real crisis, and to think: I suppose I am. That's unsettling.

Maya Delacroix did not think of herself as a master of anything. She thought of herself as someone who had learned to ask better questions. The questions she was asking now — about architecture, about organizational strategy, about what FinTechFlow needed to be competitive in three years — were better questions than she'd been asking eighteen months ago. In eighteen months, she expected them to be better again.

Keisha Williams, who had been doing this the longest, put it most plainly to a junior manager who asked her how you know when you've figured it out: "You don't figure it out. The problems get harder. What changes is how long it takes you to see what kind of problem you're looking at."

That is management mastery: not the absence of hard problems, but the speed and accuracy with which you identify them. Everything else follows from that.

The Capability Compound Effect

The thing none of them had anticipated when they started: management capabilities compound.

Maya's ability to translate between technical precision and business language — built through years of code-switching between Creole and English, between engineer and manager, between FinTechFlow and Sterling — had become her most valuable professional asset. It got her into rooms that no technical credential alone would have opened. It made her influential in policy conversations that had nothing to do with her engineering team.

David's crisis management infrastructure — the triage framework, the early warning system, the decision documentation practice his abuelo had essentially recommended years before David formalized it — had become the thing that differentiated Rodriguez Creative from other agencies its size. Clients who had been through bad experiences with agencies that fell apart under pressure chose Meridian specifically because David could demonstrate, concretely, that his operation wouldn't.

Keisha's institutional embedding methodology — born from watching her programs get dismantled and deciding to understand why rather than just be angry about it — had become a framework that Sterling Financial was implementing across nine facilities. She had turned a personal failure into an organizational capability. That was the compound: the harder the original problem, the more durable the solution.

What They Got Wrong Along the Way

David got the taco principle wrong for five years. He got the early warning system wrong for four. He got the scaling decision wrong for four months before he corrected it. Each mistake had a real cost: Cameron's eight months of undermanaged decline, three engineers who left before he'd built the retention conversation practice, the GlobalTech crisis that was partly preventable.

Maya got the delegation wrong at least four times before she got it right. She got the Connor hire and the Brett situation wrong. She got the team chemistry read wrong for two months. Each time the cost was real: a team that waited for her to solve things, a collaborative culture that took three months to rebuild, a trust deficit she had to earn back person by person.

Keisha got the knowledge transfer wrong for three years. She got the sustainability question wrong and found out after she left. She built programs that were excellent and fragile and lost them, and had to sit with that loss before she understood it well enough to build differently.

These are not footnotes. They are the education. Management mastery does not come from doing things correctly. It comes from doing things incorrectly in ways that teach you what correct actually means. The people who develop fastest as managers are not the ones who make the fewest mistakes. They're the ones who extract the most learning from the mistakes they make.

The Next Generation Problem

All three of them were now developing other managers, which turned out to be harder than developing individual contributors.

David was mentoring Zoe, who had been promoted to creative director and was navigating the peer-to-leader transition exactly the way he had — by being charming about everything and conflict-averse about the hard things. He recognized the pattern from the inside. Naming it to her was useful. Watching her work through it herself, which was the only way it actually got resolved, was harder than he'd expected.

Maya was developing two engineering leads who had different problems: one who moved too fast and broke things that mattered, and one who moved too slowly and let things break by inaction. She was trying to give them frameworks without giving them her frameworks specifically, because her frameworks were built for her context and her instincts and might not fit. She was learning that developing managers requires you to teach the thinking rather than the answers, which is significantly harder than teaching the answers.

Keisha was preparing the person who would eventually succeed her in her current role. She had started on day one, which was the lesson she'd taken from the Marcus situation. She was building the institutional embedding, the documentation, the coalition, and the relationship transfer simultaneously and from the beginning. It was more work than managing the operation. She had come to believe it was the more important work.

The Mastery Paradox

Mastery does not make leadership easier. David had been waiting for it to get easier since year three. It did not get easier. The problems got harder and his ability to handle them got better. Those two things moved in parallel without converging.

Maya had expected that at some point the translation work would become automatic. It had not. The translation layer between engineering and business had become faster and more accurate. It was still work, every time, with every audience, in every board meeting.

Keisha had expected that the institutional knowledge she'd accumulated would eventually cover most situations. It covered more situations than it used to. New situations kept appearing.

The paradox: mastery is not a destination. It's a rate of learning. The most effective managers are not the ones who know the most. They're the ones who learn the fastest from the situations they haven't encountered before. Everything they've built — the frameworks, the instincts, the guide relationships, the documentation practices — serves that one underlying capability. The speed and quality of learning under uncertainty. That is the thing worth developing.

What They'd Tell Their Earlier Selves

David would tell himself, at the beginning: the taco principle is not a management philosophy. Build the infrastructure before you need it, not after it fails you.

Maya would tell herself: people-first, problem-second, every time. Not as a step you get through. As the real conversation. Also: the gap between paper and actual is large and you will keep underestimating it.

Keisha would tell herself: build for succession from the first day, not the last. An organization that depends on one person to function isn't an organization. Also: document the counterfactual. The value of preventive work is invisible until it stops.

None of them would tell their earlier selves to avoid the hard situations. The hard situations were the education. They would just tell themselves to pay closer attention while they were in them.

Your Leadership Development Path

Focus on the rate of learning, not the accumulation of techniques. Techniques are answers to questions you've already encountered. The rate of learning determines how you handle questions you haven't.

Build your guide relationships early. Find your Sarah Braddock, your Carla, your Loretta Fines — people who have done this longer than you and will tell you what you're getting wrong. Those relationships are worth more than any management book, including this one.

When something goes wrong, extract the maximum available learning before you move on. The cost of the failure is already paid. The only variable is how much you get for it.

Maya, David, and Keisha started as reluctant managers with the wrong instincts for the job they'd been given. They're not exceptional. They're representative of what happens when people pay attention to the right things, find the right guides, and stay honest with themselves about what they're getting wrong.

You can do the same thing. The only requirement is paying attention.

Conclusion: The Management Journey Never Ends

Three people. Fourteen chapters. A lot of mistakes.

What Matters

If you've read this far, you've probably recognized yourself in at least one of these stories. Maybe you're the technical expert who got promoted and is discovering that your best skills don't transfer the way you expected. Maybe you're the manager who's been winging it in a stable environment and can feel the stability ending. Maybe you're the institutional builder watching your work get dismantled by someone who makes reasonable decisions with different priorities.

All three of those are hard. All three are survivable. None of them are what most management books prepare you for.

What Maya, David, and Keisha figured out, separately and by different routes, was the same thing: the capabilities that determined their effectiveness weren't the ones in the job description. They were the ones that developed through the situations that almost broke them. The judgment to know what kind of problem they were looking at. The discipline to address things before they became crises. The honesty to name their own avoidance before trying to assess a situation clearly.

Those capabilities are not taught. They're built. The building happens in the hard situations, through the mistakes, in the conversations you've been putting off. The building is the job.

The Development Reality

The management development that made all three of them effective was messier and more emotionally costly than any leadership program would describe.

David's crisis management capability was built through experiencing organizational failure that nearly ended his career. Maya's strategic thinking was developed through an acquisition that threatened her team's existence. Keisha's institutional sustainability methodology came from watching four years of her work get dismantled in six months.

None of these were experiences they would have chosen. All of them were formative in ways that comfortable management couldn't have produced. The capability that comes from being stretched past your current limit is different in kind from the capability that comes from training. It lives differently in you. It's available under pressure in a way that theoretical knowledge often isn't.

This is not an argument for seeking out disasters. It's an argument for paying close attention when they find you.

What This Means for You

If you're early in your management career: the challenges you're facing now are building the capabilities you'll need for the harder ones ahead. The Alex meeting Maya didn't handle well prepared her for the acquisition conversation she needed to handle well. The five-fire week David survived prepared him for the conversations he now has with managers he's developing. The failures are the curriculum.

If you're an experienced manager: the capabilities you've developed through hard situations are more transferable than you think, and more valuable than you may be communicating. The judgment you've built is the thing that's genuinely hard to develop and genuinely rare. Don't undersell it. Don't assume it's obvious.

For both: find your guides. Sarah Braddock, Carla, Loretta Fines — the real versions of those people exist in your industry and your organization. They're usually willing to talk to people who ask direct questions and demonstrate they can hear honest answers. Find them before you need them. The value of a guide relationship is highest when you're not in crisis, because that's when you can actually think.

The Journey Continues

The title of this book promises management wisdom. The honest version of that promise is: here are three people who made most of the mistakes you will make, found the frameworks that helped them, and came out the other side with capabilities they couldn't have built any other way.

The sticky note is still on Maya's monitor. People-first, problem-second. Coffee-stained, curled at the corner. She's been Engineering Director for two years and she still needs the reminder sometimes.

David still calls his abuelo when something is hard. The old man's advice is always either obvious or cryptic, and it's always right in retrospect. David has stopped being surprised by this.

Keisha still talks to Loretta Fines every few months. Loretta still doesn't waste words. The conversations are shorter than they used to be because Keisha arrives with better questions.

The management journey doesn't end. The problems get harder. The rate of learning is what you control. Pay attention. Build the infrastructure before you need it. Find your guides. Have the uncomfortable conversation earlier than is comfortable.

That's the whole thing. It's enough.

About the Author

Richard Lowe brings an unusual combination of technical expertise and storytelling mastery to the world of management writing. With 45+ years of professional experience spanning Fortune 500 technology leadership, emergency response, and creative industries, Richard understands management challenges from the ground up.

His career began in an era when computers required genuine expertise — when starting a system meant flipping physical switches in correct binary sequences and hand-coding assembly language was standard practice. As Director of Computer Operations at Trader Joe's for nearly two decades, Richard managed technology infrastructure supporting a $16 billion retail operation with 474+ stores and over 38,000 employees. He led two major digital transformations, built disaster recovery systems, and learned that managing technology was easy compared to managing the people who used it.

Richard's management education came through spectacular failures and hard-won successes: crisis situations that nearly destroyed teams, difficult personalities that tested every leadership theory, and organizational chaos that taught him the difference between management books and management reality. His insights about leadership were forged through acquisition pressures, layoff decisions, regulatory investigations, and enough interpersonal drama to fill several seasons of a workplace comedy.

As a premier ghostwriter with 113+ published books, Richard has helped clients secure over $30 million in venture capital, land TEDx speaking opportunities, and transform careers from overlooked managers to recognized industry leaders. His unique background spans cybersecurity expertise (KnowBe4 Technical Editor), academic recognition (Purdue University textbook adoption), and creative excellence (950,000+ professional photographs).

This multi-domain authority allows Richard to serve clients that traditional specialists cannot: technology executives who need both technical credibility and storytelling skills, industry leaders who demand operational accuracy with compelling narrative, and managers who require practical frameworks rather than theoretical approaches.

Richard has appeared on 55+ podcasts including The Chris Voss Show (1+ million listeners) and hosts "Leaders and Their Stories," featuring nearly 100 episodes with tech founders, executives, and changemakers. His insights about management have been featured in industry publications and conference presentations, though he's learned that the most valuable management wisdom rarely translates well into motivational quotes.

He holds certifications in emergency response (CERT-LA), has survived multiple natural disasters including three 7.1+ magnitude earthquakes and four hurricanes, and maintains a comprehensive Code of Ethics that establishes professional standards exceeding industry requirements. His real education in leadership came from working with brilliant people who taught him that the best managers are usually the ones who understand how much they still don't know.

Richard currently lives in Florida, having learned that the management skills required for surviving teenage children are surprisingly applicable to professional leadership challenges. His approach combines systems thinking from technology leadership, visual storytelling from professional photography, and the hard-earned wisdom that comes from making every management mistake at least once.

Books by Richard Lowe

See books by Richard Lowe at
https://masterofworlds.com

Get free publishing insights and industry updates at
https://thewritingking.substack.com

For ghostwriting and book coaching services see
https://thewritingking.com

Appendix: The StoryBrand Architecture of This Book

This appendix is for readers who want to understand how the book was built, and for ghostwriting clients who want to see the StoryBrand framework mapped explicitly to a complete manuscript.

StoryBrand, developed by Donald Miller, identifies seven narrative elements that appear in every compelling story. In business nonfiction, these elements are applied not to entertain but to ensure the reader remains oriented, engaged, and moving toward a transformation. What follows is the chapter-by-chapter map of how each element was deployed in this book.

The Framework Elements

HERO: The character facing the problem. In this book, the reader is always the primary hero. Maya, David, and Keisha are secondary heroes who model the path. VILLAIN: The force working against the hero. In management nonfiction, the villain is rarely a person — it's a pattern, a gap, a structural problem. STAKES: What is lost if the villain wins. GUIDE: The character who arrives with a framework. Guides have credibility and empathy — they've been where the hero is and they know the way out. PLAN: The specific, named methodology the guide provides. CALL TO ACTION: The behavior change the reader is asked to make. TRANSFORMATION: The before and after that shows the hero changed.

Chapter-by-Chapter Map

CHAPTER 1 (Maya). Hero: Maya Delacroix, newly promoted engineering team lead. Villain: Her own engineering instincts applied to human problems — the impulse to debug people like broken systems. Stakes: Team fractures in 90 days; every voice that said she was too junior is proven right. Guide: Sarah Braddock, former manager, now VP. Plan: People-first, problem-second. Every time. Find out what someone is experiencing before you diagnose or propose. Transformation: From engineer who treats people as unreliable systems to manager who builds conditions for people to do their best work.

CHAPTER 2 (David). Hero: David Rodriguez, five years into managing a creative team on instinct. Villain: The absence of management infrastructure — the taco principle as a substitute for a real operating system. Stakes: Loses the team's confidence, loses his boss's confidence, loses a major client. Guide: Carla, new department head. Plan: Minimum viable infrastructure. Categorize decisions by reversibility and blast radius. Communicate upward as strategic consultation, not status reporting. Transformation: From manager who wings it in stable conditions to manager with systems that function under pressure.

CHAPTER 3 (Maya). Hero: Maya hiring her first engineer. Villain: The credential trap — hiring for the job description she already wrote instead of the future she can't fully predict. Stakes: One bad hire compounds across the whole team; the team's capability moves in the wrong direction. Guide: Sarah Braddock. Plan: Hire for learning trajectory and collaborative capacity. Test for how candidates handle being wrong, not just whether they know the right answers. Investigate references rather than confirming them. Transformation: From hiring for yesterday's problems to hiring for tomorrow's challenges.

CHAPTER 4 (Keisha). Hero: Keisha Williams, fifteen years of operations management expertise meeting a matrix restructure. Villain: The limits of a relationship-based influence network that doesn't scale to new organizational scope. Stakes: Coordination failures in crises, loss of influence with new stakeholders, inability to do the job she was given. Guide: Loretta Fines, retired predecessor. Plan: Map the informal network explicitly. Calibrate communication to each executive's information style. Build influence by making other people more successful before asking for cooperation. Transformation: From departmental manager with deep informal influence to organizational coordinator with systematic reach.

CHAPTER 5 (David). Hero: David managing performance on a stable team. Villain: The output/performance confusion — tracking deliverables instead of the trajectory behind them. Stakes: Cameron's slow decline goes undetected for eight months; a client flags it before David does. Guide: Carla. Plan: Track trajectory, not just output. Diagnose capability gaps vs. effort problems before intervening. Structure difficult conversations as collaborative diagnosis rather than corrective judgment. Transformation: From output-tracker to performance developer.

CHAPTER 6 (Maya). Hero: Maya managing team chemistry after the Brett Callahan hire. Villain: The invisible tax Brett introduces on collaborative culture — technically excellent, organizationally corrosive. Stakes: Team trust degrades over three months; collaborative culture that took a year to build is damaged in weeks. Guide: Sarah Braddock. Plan: People-reading practice — watch how individuals change relative to themselves over time. Three-question personnel decision framework: willing to adapt in practice? Cost to team of continued investment? Waiting because change is coming or because decision is uncomfortable? Transformation: From manager who addresses personnel problems when they're undeniable to manager who detects them when they're still recoverable.

CHAPTER 7 (Keisha). Hero: Keisha discovering she has made herself a single point of failure. Villain: Indispensability — the institutional knowledge trap that makes an excellent manager irreplaceable and therefore unscalable. Stakes: Can't take a vacation, can't be promoted, organization collapses around any gap in her presence. Guide: Loretta Fines. Plan: Three-layer documentation. Decision authority distribution with intentional withdrawal. Relationship transfer through substantive introductions. Loretta's question: if you left tomorrow, what would break? Work the list. Transformation: From indispensable individual to builder of organizational capability.

CHAPTER 8 (David). Hero: David working under Victoria Brennan, a boss who undermines his authority publicly. Villain: Victoria's management style and the power asymmetry it creates. Stakes: David's authority erodes, his team loses confidence in him, his professional reputation depends entirely on Victoria's account of his work. Guide: The abuelo. Plan: Preemptive influence — shape decisions before they're made. Build organizational relationships that exist independently of the reporting line. Keep factual records. Outlast or leave; do it with dignity. Transformation: From manager who believes good work speaks for itself to manager who actively manages his professional presence and reputation.

CHAPTER 9 (Maya). Hero: Maya leading her team through FinTechFlow's acquisition by Sterling Financial. Villain: Acquisition economics — Sterling's financial logic, which evaluates her team as cost rather than capability. Stakes: 40% of the engineering team faces redundancy; the culture Maya built is irrelevant to the acquiring company's calculus. Guide: Sarah Braddock. Plan: Build the irreplaceable case before it's needed. Lead with what the acquiring organization needs to know. Translate cultural integration as bilingualism, not submission. Manage the team's emotional experience alongside the strategic positioning. Transformation: From team lead operating within a stable organization to senior manager navigating organizational survival and strategic repositioning.

CHAPTER 10 (David). Hero: David scaling Meridian's creative team under GlobalTech contract pressure. Villain: The personal leadership model that works at twelve people and fails at twenty-four. Stakes: Contract performance penalties, client relationship at risk, team quality degrading under a leader operating past his capacity limit. Guide: Carla. Plan: Scale leadership infrastructure alongside headcount. Hire for chaos tolerance under time pressure. Move from decision-maker to builder of decision-makers. The signal you've delegated correctly: being surprised by good decisions made without you. Transformation: From intimate team leader to organizational builder who leads through structure rather than personal involvement.

CHAPTER 11 (Keisha). Hero: Keisha watching her programs get dismantled after her promotion. Villain: The sustainability illusion — programs that were excellent and personal, dependent on Keisha's presence to function. Stakes: Four years of professional work effectively reversed within six months of departure. Guide: Loretta Fines, and Keisha's grandmother. Plan: Structural embedding (in job descriptions, performance metrics, budget allocations). Coalition building (stakeholders on record as advocates). Counterfactual documentation (what this program prevents, not just what it produces). Transformation: From builder of excellent programs to builder of institutional capabilities that survive leadership transitions.

CHAPTER 12 (Maya). Hero: Maya as newly promoted Engineering Director. Villain: Team lead instincts applied to director-level responsibilities — technical framing for organizational decisions, project-time thinking for organizational-time problems. Stakes: Board loses confidence; engineering investment not connecting to business strategy; retention conversations too reactive to retain key people. Guide: Sarah Braddock. Plan: Build the business case alongside the technical recommendation. Have trajectory conversations before engineers are restless. Say yes to the industry invitations — your reputation is an organizational asset. Think in organizational time (years), not project time (quarters). Transformation: From excellent technical manager to senior leader who connects engineering capability to organizational strategy.

CHAPTER 13 (David). Hero: David facing five simultaneous crises in a single week. Villain: Compounding failure — not five separate problems but an interconnected system of failures each making the others worse. Stakes: GlobalTech account, legal exposure, team stability, budget, and David's own credibility all threatened simultaneously. Guide: The abuelo. Carla (post-crisis debrief). Plan: Triage by type (legal/HR first, business-critical second, important-but-not-urgent third, everything else waits). Address what's making the other things worse first. Build early warning systems: what's developing that I don't know about yet? Transformation: From manager who handles problems as they become undeniable to manager with detection systems and triage frameworks for crises that develop slowly.

CHAPTER 14 and CONCLUSION. The final chapter closes all three arcs and articulates the underlying insight that connects them: mastery is not the absence of hard problems. It's the speed and accuracy with which you identify what kind of problem you're looking at. The conclusion returns to the reader as primary hero and offers the three things that accelerated Maya, David, and Keisha's development: a framework for each type of challenge, a guide relationship, and the discipline to extract maximum learning from situations that were going to be costly either way.

For Ghostwriting Clients

The StoryBrand architecture in this book was applied at three levels simultaneously: chapter level (each chapter has its own complete hero arc), series level (the three characters' arcs develop across chapters and intersect at key points), and book level (the reader's transformation from uncertain manager to capable leader is the macro arc that everything else serves).

This layered application is what separates StoryBrand as a structural methodology from StoryBrand as a marketing technique. The framework is not a formula — it's a set of questions that, answered well, produce writing that readers experience as a story even when the content is practical nonfiction.

I apply this methodology to every book I ghostwrite for clients who want their nonfiction to be read rather than purchased and shelved. If you're evaluating this book as a sample of that work, the architecture above is the deliverable. The prose is how it was executed.

Contact: thewritingking.com